# MUSSOLINI
## THE MAN OF DESTINY

## IL DUCE

Wearing his Fascist Leader's uniform when he presented himself before
the King after the March on Rome

# MUSSOLINI
## THE MAN OF DESTINY

BY

VITTORIO E. DE FIORI

*Translated from the Italian*

BY

MARIO A. PEI

ILLUSTRATED

LONDON AND TORONTO
J. M. DENT & SONS, LTD.

# CONTENTS

## PART ONE

[ v ]

# Contents

# Contents

# Contents

# Contents

# LIST OF ILLUSTRATIONS

[ xi ]

# List of Illustrations

# THE AUTHOR

VOLUMES have been written about Mussolini. Rivers of ink have flowed for and against the man who in so short a time has risen to a predominant position among the political giants of the world. Authorized biographers have attempted to portray his complex personality. All have tried to say something new about him, but their accounts have been, for the most part, hazy, confused, partisan, and interspersed with a variety of considerations and criticisms which can be of no possible interest to the American reader.

The only one who has succeeded in giving us a definite, well-balanced idea of the Italian Premier's past life is the author of this biography. While much has been said about the Italian Dictator since he seized the reins of government, very little is known about his past life as a politician, a journalist and a private man. Vittorio E. De Fiori fills this gap and presents "il Duce" to the American public in chronological order, from his birth to his ascent to power.

Mr. De Fiori is eminently fitted to narrate the life of Benito Mussolini, for he was intimately associated with him for many years. In the following pages he presents a graphic, entertaining series of pen pictures describing the intimate, personal life of the Man of Destiny upon whom are centered the eyes of the entire world.

Mr. De Fiori, the son of a noted Italian physician, was born in Venice, Italy. He graduated from Tito Livio College and later attended the University of Padua. At the age of eighteen he volunteered and served in the Italian Army, and since then has been actively interested in the affairs of the Italian nation. He taught modern languages in two of Italy's leading colleges before entering the newspaper field. His first journalistic venture was as a correspondent for "Turlu-pineide," a Vicenza publication. From Switzerland, where he first became intimately acquainted with the future Premier, he wrote articles for Italian newspapers and magazines. Upon his return to Italy he joined the staff of Mussolini's paper, "Il Popolo d'Italia."

In America Mr. De Fiori has been further identified with the journalistic world, first as founder of the "Rinascenza Italica," an anti-Red publication, and later as editor of "Il Messaggero" of New York, N. Y. The latter was the first and only newspaper in America to publish Mussolini's War Diary, and many other articles sent to the editor by Mussolini himself.

Mr. De Fiori is one of the few original founders of the Fascist movement in this country, which has for its purpose to give the Italian immigrants a better understanding of American ideals and to combat all forms of subversivism.

THE TRANSLATOR.

[ xv ]

# FOREWORD

MR. DE FIORI'S acquaintance and newspaper association with Mussolini, before his rise to power, has enabled him to understand his character and his career as few others could do.

I believe that a great many intelligent Americans, and the very great number of Italians in the United States, would want to read this book.

The facts in it will be extremely interesting in future history.

ARTHUR BRISBANE

*In 1912, George Sorel, the great French revolutionary philosopher, had written about Mussolini:*

"Our Mussolini is not an ordinary Socialist. It is my belief that some day we shall see him at the head of a mighty legion, saluting the Italian flag with his sword. He is a Fifteenth Century Italian, a Condottiero. He does not yet know it himself, but he is the only man of energy in Italy who can save the country from its government's fundamental weakness."

"Fascism is a typically Italian product, just as Bolshevism is typically Russian. Neither of the two can be transplanted or live outside of its native land."

MUSSOLINI.

# MUSSOLINI
## THE MAN OF DESTINY

### PART ONE

# CHAPTER I: THE EARLY YEARS

THE character of the inhabitants of the Romagna district has been described as cruelly somber. The character of Benito Mussolini, on the other hand, may be defined as cruelly sentimental.

His bad temper is evident on all occasions, in love and in hatred, at work and at play. His large, deep, penetrating eyes, ready to defend or assail, appear full of perpetual anger. At rare intervals they become kind and tranquil, and at such times they seem to lie at peace in a sea of phosphorus, smiling quietly, like the large eyes of a child. However, these are only brief intervals of peace in a life replete with quick, violent changes and sudden, explosive ideas, mastered emotions and unbridled desires, instants of repose, as it were, in a busy workshop where repose is the exception, not the rule.

Benito Mussolini was born, on July 29, 1883, in the village of Dovia, municipality of Predappio, province of Forlì, Romagna. No star, as far as can be ascertained, predicted a brilliant destiny for him at the time.

His mother, Rosa Maltoni, to whom Mussolini ascribes his iron character, was an austere woman, accustomed to regard the good qualities and virtues of the people around her with reverence. She was an elementary school teacher at a time when school teachers in Italy were paid like and looked upon as servants. Her wretched salary, during periods of financial straits, which were quite frequent in the Mussolini household, was barely sufficient to provide the immediate necessities of life. She was occasionally compelled to have recourse to the authorities for a subsidy. One of her letters, addressed to the prefect of the province of Forlì, in which she asked for a bonus that would enable her to continue the education of her son Benito, reads as follows:

"Ever mindful of the day when Your Excellency deigned to visit my school, and recalling that on that occasion Your Excellency was good enough to express a flattering opinion about me, saying that my long years of service entitled me to a bonus from the Minister of Education, I take the liberty to remind your Excellency of those kind words.

"As Your Excellency undoubtedly knows, economic conditions in this town are quite bad this year, owing to the disastrous harvest and the total failure of the grape crop. Because of this, my family is in such a state that I shall soon be compelled to withdraw from the Royal Normal School of Forlimpopoli our twelve-year-old son Benito, who, according to his instructors, shows some promise. I shall be everlastingly grateful if

[ 5 ]

Your Excellency will be kind enough to propose me for a bonus or advise me as to how I may obtain a subsidy for my son, or aid me in any way."

Needless to say, this petition remained unanswered, and is still filed away in the archives of the Prefecture of Forlì, with the number 1920/8 and the annotation "Refused."

She taught her children to look upon poverty as a form of aristocracy, and to be proud of it. Mussolini still recalls some of his mother's maxims and repeats them to his friends:

"Learn to live without everything that seems essential to your comfort, but if you come across someone who is in want, give him, if you can, twice as much as he needs."

"Nobility of the spirit is the only true nobility. It sets you apart from the common herd."

It is undoubtedly to his mother that Mussolini owes the rigid sense of superiority and aristocracy in poverty which has always been one of his predominant characteristics.

His father, Alessandro Mussolini, was, on the contrary, a violent, rebellious man, whose hatred for social injustice made him one of the fiercest international revolutionists of his day. He named his son Benito, after Benito Juarez, the Mexican revolutionist and president, who was directly responsible for the execution of Emperor Maximilian.

The Mussolini family had its origin in Bologna , about the year 1430. The Mussolinis were, in former times, politicians and leaders of the people. In Bologna there is still a Mussolini street, and up to a century ago there still existed a Mussolini tower and a Mussolini square. It is not without reason, therefore, that Mussolini loves to call himself a "son of the people."

From the age of six till he was nine, Benito attended elementary school. He was an aggressive, turbulent urchin, who frequently came home with his head cut open by a rocky missile, his face swollen and scratched or his eyes blackened. But even then he knew how to take care of himself, and now he almost boasts of the fact that in his boyhood he was a holy terror.

Like all bad boys, he had a special fancy for birds. Once he stole a thrush that served as a decoy for hunting parties. Hotly pursued by the angry proprietor, he ran down a hill, through fields and meadows, and finally had to swim across a river, but he never relinquished his booty.

He was gluttonous, too. One day, after gorging himself with pilfered cherries, he stained his face with the juice of the few that remained on the tree, and ran through the streets of the town, shouting and crying desperately as if in severe pain. People came running in alarm at the sight of what they thought was blood, but Benito, foreseeing the plenteous spanking that would befall him if his trick were discovered, hastened

MUSSOLINI AT THE AGE OF 14

off with a mocking gesture at his would-be rescuers.

A gang of boys of which Benito was the leader decided to steal quinces from a tree belonging to a notoriously stingy old farmer. While the operation was in progress, the irate owner was seen striding toward the thieves with a knotted stick raised in his clenched fist. The boys took to their heels, but one of them, in his haste to jump from the tree, fractured his ankle. Benito had been among the first to run, but when he heard the pitiful cries of his disabled comrade he ran back, picked him up and hastened off again in the nick of time.

His mother occasionally tried to take him to church, but Benito could not remain there long, especially during lengthy, tedious services. The feeble light of the candles, the penetrating odor of the incense, the monotonous singing of the psalms and the deep-toned voice of the organ seemed to have a strange, perturbing effect upon him.

Nevertheless, his mother insisted upon giving him a religious education and decided to send him to a Salesian boarding school. His father vehemently objected at first, but later yielded to his wife's wishes.

During the week that preceded his departure, Benito was worse than ever. A great restlessness seemed to have come over him. He thought a boarding school was a variety of prison. Taking advantage of the last few days of liberty he had left, he gave free rein to his ardent temperament and roamed up and down the streets, through fields, woods and vineyards laden with luscious grapes.

# CHAPTER II: MUSSOLINI THE STUDENT

FINALLY everything was in readiness. His sorrow at parting from his sister Edvige, then three, and his brother Arnaldo, then seven, was surpassed by his anxiety about his pet canary, which he kept in a bright, shining cage by the window of his little room. At the very moment of departure his eyes filled with tears, and as he climbed into the donkey-cart he issued a last recommendation about the canary to his mother.

His father whipped up the donkey and the journey began. They had barely gone two hundred yards when the animal stumbled and fell. "That's a bad sign!" murmured his father, as he helped the donkey to regain its

[ 11 ]

feet. There were no further incidents, but Benito kept silent. His large eyes followed the swallows in their free flight with a deep, uncontrollable feeling of nostalgia. With a repressed sob he heard the gurgling murmur of the brook that seemed to bid him good-bye.

They passed through Forlì. The sight of the city brought back a memory to his mind: once, when four years old, he had been lost there and was found, several hours later, seated before the door of a shoemaker's shop, gravely puffing at the stub of a Tuscan cigar that the generous shoemaker had bestowed upon him.

Night was falling when they came to Faenza and knocked at the door of the Salesian boarding school. Benito was received by the rector, a limping, unctuous little old priest who, placing his hand on the boy's head, said with a kindly smile: "He must be a very lively boy." How correct his estimate was, the good priest was very soon to find out.

His father kissed him good-bye and left. When he found himself alone with the rector, Benito could no longer restrain himself and burst into tears.

But his stay at the boarding school was destined to be brief. Restless and arrogant, he frequently argued and occasionally got into fights with his companions. He was severely reprimanded and punished, but to no avail. Finally he was expelled.

His disappointed parents placed him in another institution nearer home. There, too, Benito proved to be anything but a saint. He was headstrong and incorrigible, and was tolerated only because of his remarkable intelligence. The school inspector, who was a brother of Carducci, once jokingly said to him: "You are a very bright boy. If you don't stop, you will be a State Minister at thirty."

He was forever breaking rules and regulations. One night a concert was being given in Verdi's honor at the municipal theatre.

Benito applied for permission to attend it, but was refused. This did not discourage him in the least. With the aid of a companion, he used the bedsheets as a rope, let himself down from a window, went to the theatre, had an excellent time, and when he was quite ready got back into the dormitory by the same means by which he had left it and went to bed.

In spite of his restlessness, he was always a good student. He had an intense fondness for study, but he was invariably a rebel to school routine. At an oral examination he was asked a question to which he replied with a half-hour speech on a topic of his own choice. He received a zero, but his examiners were astounded at his precocious oratorical ability.

At the age of eleven, during the holidays, his mother surprised him in his room, where he was frantically orating and gesticulating.

"What is the matter with you, Benito?" she asked in alarm.

"Hush, mother, I'm making a speech. When I grow up all of Italy will throb at my words!"

Benito's adolescence was tempestuous and replete with incidents. His nature, rebellious to routine and pedantry, found an outlet in daring, youthful day-dreams. In school he was forever writing the word "Rome" on all his books and papers, in an infinite variety of scripts and dimensions. His spirit was irresistibly attracted by the fascination of the Eternal City.

However, he made his first pleasure trip to Ravenna, with his mother, and was subdued by the austerity of the tomb of Dante and the beauty of the church of Saint Apollinaris. In Ravenna his dreamer's soul was completely won over by the mystery of art.

As a student he was never the first in the class. His vivacity often made him listless and inattentive. But at the age of fifteen he received his normal school license at Forlimpopoli and felt fully entitled to make his first literary attempts.

His impetuous tendencies were the cause of his failing to obtain an appointment as municipal secretary. His father waxed bitterly resentful over the fact, and addressed the town council with these prophetic words:

"The same thing will happen to you that happened to the Council of Palermo, which refused Crispi as its secretary. My son is destined to go a long way. You will see!"

The conscript fathers of Predappio were probably afraid that young Mussolini, in the post of secretary, would shake the quiet municipality out of its century-old slumber, and they were probably not altogether wrong.

Later, after many fruitless attempts, Benito finally obtained an appointment as an elementary school teacher in Gualtieri, a town on the banks of the Po. The following year he was transferred to Oneglia, on the Ligurian Riviera.

# CHAPTER III: MUSSOLINI THE EXILE

TO SEE THE WORLD—SWITZERLAND AND HOMESICKNESS
—POVERTY AND HUNGER—A BEGGAR AND A TRAMP

But this rebellious student and teacher hated the cramped, confining atmosphere of schools. And so, one fine day in 1902, yielding to his restless wanderlust, he packed up his few belongings, boarded a train without even saying good-bye to his friends, and left the country.

He wanted to observe, study, work, turn the world upside down; he didn't know exactly what he wanted. He was simply out to breathe the bracing air of freedom.

When he reached Chiasso, while waiting for the train that was to take him to French Switzerland, he bought a copy of the Milan "Secolo" and read, to his grief and astonishment, that his father had been arrested. The Predappio Socialists, in an effort to prevent the victory of the Clericals, had smashed the ballot-boxes. The authorities had arrested several of the ringleaders, Alessandro Mussolini among them.

Benito hesitated, torn between conflicting desires to proceed and to return home. He finally decided to continue his journey, though he had but two lire and twenty centimes in his pocket.

His first experiences as an exile are graphically recounted in a letter which he wrote to a friend:

". . . and so I boarded the train that was to take me to Lucerne: a twelve hour trip. The coach was full of Italians, fellow-exiles. I spent almost the entire time at the window. It was a splendid night, with the moon rising among silvery stars, behind lofty mountains that were white with snow. The Lake of Lugano gleamed with magic reflections, like a smooth metallic surface struck by fairy lights. Mount Gotthard was like a thoughtful, kindly giant, making a way for the steel serpent that was swiftly bearing me away to another land.

"Everybody slept in the coach. I alone sat thinking. What was I thinking of on that night that marked the dividing line between two periods of my life? I don't remember. In the morning, as we entered German Switzerland, and a dreary November rain coldly greeted us, I recalled the green meadows of Italy, kissed by the fiery rays of the southern sun, and a pang of weariness and homesickness shot through my heart.

"At Lucerne I changed trains for Yverdon. When I got there, tired and dazed, I turned my steps toward a miserable tavern where, for the first time, I had occasion to make use of the French I had learned in school.

"The following day I found a job as a bricklayer's assistant: eleven hours of work a day, thirty-two centimes an hour. I made

121 trips with a load of bricks to the second story of a house under construction. That night the muscles of my arms were so swollen and sore that I could barely touch them. I ate some potatoes roasted in the ashes and threw myself, dressed as I was, upon my bed, a heap of straw. At five in the morning I got up and went back to work. I quivered with impotent anger. The sight of the boss, with his fat, smug, self-satisfied face, gave me hydrophobia. On the third day he said to me: 'You're too well-dressed.' He meant that to be significant. I felt like rebelling and breaking the head of that newly-rich peasant who accused me of being lazy while my bones were cracking under the strain. But what if I had done it? The employer is always in the right.

"When the end of the week came, I told the boss that I was going to leave and wanted my pay. He went into his office while I waited outside on the landing. When he came out he angrily thrust twenty-odd francs into my hand and snarled: 'Here you are; it's stolen money!' I was too dumbfounded to reply. What should I have done? Killed him? As a matter of fact, I turned away in silence. I was hungry and barefooted. A pair of almost new shoes that I had brought with me had been torn to shreds on the rocks and bricks that had cut their way into my hands, my feet and my soul. I hurried off to an Italian store-keeper and bought a pair of hobnailed shoes. The next morning I left for Lausanne."

He reached Lausanne without a penny in his pocket. All day long he sought work in vain. Night came on, and still he was unemployed. He was hungry.

It is only when one is in a strange country, far from home, alone, penniless and homesick, that one realizes how much strength of character it takes to refrain from bursting into tears like a child.

Mussolini trudged on silently and sullenly, along a deserted road. Suddenly, as in a fairy tale, he saw a light ahead of him. He drew near. It was a modest kitchen lamp that shed its beams upon a tranquil domestic scene. In a farmyard, half concealed in darkness, around a dining table, sat some men, some children and a woman. It was a temptation for a heart filled with weariness and sullen anger, and for a stomach that had long been empty. Mussolini never resists temptations because, he says, they are too feminine. He yielded. Without humility or rudeness, resolute and clear-eyed, he entered the quiet farmyard and thrust his brigand-like eyes and dusty face into the candor of that domestic picture. Silence greeted him. Half a dozen pairs of astonished eyes were turned upon him.

"Have you some bread?" he frankly inquired.

There was no reply. Then a hand slowly picked up a loaf from the table, remained suspended for an instant in the soft light of the lamp, holding that light, yet terrible bur-

[ 22 ]

Doing His Share of Work in the Battle of the Grain

den, and handed it to the stranger, who took it quickly, almost brusquely.

"Thank you."

Silence still reigned.

"Good night."

He vanished in the darkness. The cruel sentimentalism of his character took the upper hand, clutching at his heart. He impetuously raised his arm to throw away that mendicant's loaf. Then he hesitated. His arm fell back to his side, and his dry mouth angrily bit into the bread. He ate silently, in the dark, walking more and more quickly, closing his eyes from time to time, as if to shut out the vision of that lamp, that hand, and that silent table.

# CHAPTER IV: MUSSOLINI THE VAGABOND

THE CALL OF THE UNKNOWN—"A BULWARK OF
BAYONETS"—A HAUGHTY VAGRANT

THE roadways of the world drew him on
with their irresistible lure. Many still recall
the time when he fought his hard, daily battle for bread. He worked for years as a
mason's assistant, station porter, weaver, and
butcher's boy. From time to time he was discharged because of one of his customary acts
of rebellion against discipline and restraint.
Then long intervals of vagrancy would ensue.
But his vagrancy was intellectual. The unemployed rebel would become a temporary
student at some university. His spirit was
athirst for knowledge.

From Switzerland he passed on to France,
Germany and Austria, studying the people

of each country he lived in and learning their languages. Finally he came back to Italy to see his mother and serve in the army. He was assigned to the Bersaglieri, Italy's crack light infantry corps. It was at this time that the greatest sorrow in his life came to him. His mother died. But he was strong even in the midst of his grief. In his reply to a letter of sympathy sent him by his captain, he said:

"On behalf of my father, my sister and my brother, I wish to thank you, and with you all of my superiors and comrades, for the kind words with which you have tried to alleviate my sorrow. As you say, Captain, the only thing that now remains for me to do is to follow my mother's advice and honor her memory by faithfully discharging all my duties as a soldier and a citizen. Women may weep and groan, but strong men must suffer and die in silence.

"In order to be able to work for the common good, and honor the sacred memories of the family and the nation, we must not give way to fruitless lamentations. It is well to commemorate the heroes whose blood has cemented the unity of Italy, but we must also prove that we are not unworthy descendants of those heroes, and that we are ready to present a mighty bulwark of breasts and bayonets when the barbarians from the north again attempt to reduce Italy to a geographic expression."

Shortly after he had completed his military service, he left for Switzerland again to resume his intellectual vagabondage.

One night he found himself alone, hungry and penniless, as usual. It was one of those moments in a man's life when the most beautiful surroundings make a gloomy, dismal impression. The sound of happy voices in the streets got on his nerves. The lights gleaming in every window irritated him. The tables of restaurants, with their shining silverware and spotless linen, made him feel the pangs of hunger all the more keenly. He felt surging up within him an unconquerable hatred for the smug, prosperous city, whose gaiety seemed to mock his hunger. As his discomfort grew, he realized that there were only two courses open to him that night; either to disturb the peace and get arrested, or to crawl away and hide somewhere, like a snarling, wounded animal. He chose the latter alternative.

He wandered on till he came to a deserted bridge. He looked down, and seeing that the bed of the little stream was dry, he selected it for his shelter.

It was undoubtedly a fine bed chamber. There was plenty of fresh air and abundant light from the stars. In the distance could be heard the sounds of the happy city's merriment. Near by absolute silence prevailed, save for the chirp of a chance cricket.

He looked about for a pillow and failed to find it. Then he leaned his shoulders against the wall, drew up his knees underneath his chin, laid his head upon them, shut his eyes and waited for sleep. He waited in vain. The cricket had a great deal to say to his lady-love, and other crickets occasionally turned the duet into a chorus, their chirps coming from afar on the brisk breeze that stirred the bushes, swayed the branches and penetrated to the wanderer's marrow.

Later on the crickets were replaced by whirring swarms of mosquitoes, merrily swirling over their luscious prey. Then came the noise of doors opening and shutting, and the manifold, mysterious voices of the night borne about by the wind. Finally the gleaming stars went out and a thin, persistent rain began to fall, striking the leaves of the trees, at first with the slow rythm of a tango, then accelerating to a waltz, and lastly taking on the swift tempo of a fox-trot.

Mussolini got up. A short distance from the bridge he saw a large wooden shack that formed part of a near-by printing plant. Rest and sleep awaited him there, he thought. He scaled a window and dropped inside. There was a strong smell of paper and ink about the place, but he didn't mind that. He groped his way to a corner, lay down on a heap of paper cuttings, and fell asleep.

He slept on long after the sun had risen. When he finally opened his eyes, he saw a waiting policeman standing patiently erect at his side.

Mussolini's first waking thought was that Swiss policemen were very polite not to disturb one's sleep.

"Well?" asked the policeman.

"Well?" countered Mussolini.

"What are you doing here?"

"Supervising my printing establishment, as you see."

"Get up."

"Just a minute. Let me tell the maid to bring me my morning suit and serve my breakfast."

"Cut out the fooling. Get up, or I'll help you to."

Mussolini smiled lazily, stretched out his hand, and said:

[ 30 ]

"That will be fine; help me."

"You're Italian, aren't you?"

"Yes; export department."

"All right, come with me."

Mussolini yawned, stretched and got up to follow the minion of the law.

It was a beautiful morning. The sun shone brightly in the sky. Tempting odors of freshly baked bread and ripe fruit were borne to the vagabond's nostrils. Washer-women sang at their work in the waters of a little stream, children on their way to school thronged the streets, and laborers issued from their homes to resume their wonted tasks.

"Come on! Hustle up!"

Mussolini scowlingly followed the guardian of law and order who, unaware of the storm that raged inside the prisoner's breast, urged him on from time to time.

The passers-by gave him curious, hostile glances as he walked down the street, drawing to one side as though he had been a leper.

He was locked up in a cell, where he final-

[ 31 ]

ly found a companion. It was a horribly deformed, unbelievably filthy old man, who crouched in a dark corner and occasionally thrust his hand inside his tattered shirt.

Mussolini shuddered when the claw-like hand of the old man was fastened upon his arm.

"Who are you?" asked the old man in a voice made raucous by drink.

Mussolini turned away in disgust, without answering.

"Italian, eh?" inquired the heap of rags and filth, shaking his head and returning his bony hand to its favorite occupation. Mussolini scowled.

Then that human refuse, upon whom all parasites found hospitality, tried to be sarcastic.

"Knife business, eh?"

Mussolini could stand it no longer. With flashing eyes and a voice hoarse with indignation, he flung back:

"No, no knife! Italians don't use knives.

They only use scissors to cut their hair and nails, water to wash, and common decency to make sure they're not bothering other people!"

The vagabond of the streets, the tattered representative of vice and wretchedness, who knew no liberty save that of theft and brutishness, remained open-mouthed and gaping before the fiery anger of this strange vagabond of a new ideal.

# PART TWO

# CHAPTER V: MUSSOLINI THE UNDESIRABLE

IN Geneva Mussolini came in contact with men of letters and politics who quickly grew to admire his intelligence, ambition, and tenacity. He began to write for various Swiss and Italian publications and to lecture on Socialism and international politics. His fluent, persuasive oratory struck a responsive chord not only in the laboring masses, but even in the local bourgeoisie and intellectuals. The Swiss authorities began to notice him and keep their eyes on him.

His ideas concerning universal democracy, probably inspired by the writings of Pareto, date back to this time.

"Equality and democracy," said Mussolini in one of his most brilliant lectures, "are humanity's greatest illusions. They are ideals which, if they were put into practise, would destroy interest, beauty, and individuality in life."

It was also at this period of his life that he came into contact with the philosophies of Nietzsche and Sorel, both of whom played a very definite rôle in his spiritual formation.

While Mussolini was in Switzerland, the great French Socialist, Jaurès, came to Geneva to hold a lecture on "Christ." The lecture-hall was filled to overflowing, and Mussolini, mingling with the throng of laborers, impatiently awaited the appearance of the famous orator. Poorly dressed, with a sullen face and burning eyes, he attracted the attention of his neighbors, who thought him a violent Anarchist and eyed him with suspicion.

Shortly after Juarès had begun his lecture, Mussolini commenced to give visible and audible signs of his dissent.

"Put him out!" the crowd began to shout indignantly.

But the voice of the stranger rose above the tumult, and taking advantage of a momentary lull in the commotion, he cried out:

"I want to speak, too! I have the right to say what I think!"

For an instant the wrath of the audience seemed on the point of being translated into terms of action, but Jaurès himself called for order, assuring his unknown opponent that he would be allowed full freedom of debate as soon as the lecture was over.

When Jaurès had finished his lecture, Mussolini was invited to have his say. In the midst of a sepulchral silence, he advanced briskly to the platform, not at all daunted by the evident hostility of the audience or the personality of the great man with whom he did himself the honor of disagreeing. With the easy grace of an experienced orator, he faced the crowd and launched into a violent denunciation of the Gospel and the Galilean, who, to his mind, had been guilty of over-throwing the magnificent structure of the Roman Empire with his "slave morality," weakening, with his pacifistic ideals, the Empire's defense against the barbaric hordes that swept down from the north. Then, advancing irrefutable quotations and arguments, he went back to Buddha through Schopenhauer and Nietzsche.

"After all," he concluded, "what was the Messiah, with his few speeches and parables, in comparison with the doctrines elaborated by Buddha in forty volumes, through forty years of penance, meditation and apostolic labor?"

His words came forth clear and persuasive, permeated with such a stringent logic that Jaurès himself, after Mussolini had finished, warmly clasped his hand, congratulating him on his wonderful debate, while the audience enthusiastically applauded.

But one fine day the Swiss police, fearing that the young exponent of radical theories

MUSSOLINI AND CHAMBERLAIN

might prove a menace to the peace of the tranquil Republic, ordered his deportation from Swiss territory.

When Mussolini heard of the severe decision rendered against him by the Federal authorities, he fled to Lausanne, whence he wrote to his friend, Dr. A. Wyss, then a Socialist representative from Geneva:

"I have just read in the 'Genevois' that you intend to present a protest to the Federal Council concerning my expulsion, which was decreed by the Commissioner of Police. In order that you may be better enabled to do this, I shall present you with a brief autobiography.

"I came to Switzerland at the age of 19. I worked and earned an honest living in Lausanne. I went back to Italy to see my mother, and then with my friend Donatini, a political refugee, I fixed my residence in Annemasse, on the other side of the French border, where we planned to establish an international review of Socialistic culture.

"On March 1, 1904, I came to Geneva with the intention of registering at the University. They will tell you that I am an Anarchist. That is a lie. During these last few years I have written and lectured a good deal, contributing out of my own pocket to the support of the New York 'Proletario,' the Lugano 'Avvenire del Lavoratore' and the Milan 'Avanguardia.' I defy the police to discover a single anarchistic line in any of my writings. Both in Switzerland and in Italy, I have always been looked upon as a Socialist. At our Zurich convention I presented a motion which, though revolutionary, cannot in any way be interpreted as anarchistic.

"During the forty days I was in Geneva, I spent most of my time in the University library. The police report about me is a pack of unmitigated lies. I was deported without even being granted time to return the keys of my room, pack my belongings or consult my lawyers.

[ 42 ]

"The authorities told my lawyers that I had gone back to Annemasse. The truth is that I was compelled to board a train for Chiasso in order to be deported to Italy.

"My expulsion is a disgrace to a Republic that wishes to preserve the traditions of Swiss liberty. A similar proceeding is unworthy even of a monarchy.

"I am now in Lausanne, where I hope I shall be left undisturbed. The Commissioner of Police will have some difficulty in justifying his action."

# CHAPTER VI. MUSSOLINI THE IRREDENTIST

IN 1908 Mussolini moved to Austria and was for a short time editor of "L'Avvenire di Trento." Then he became associate editor of "Il Popolo," a daily owned and published by Cesare Battisti, who used the social issue as a means of keeping alive the Italian spirit in the inhabitants of the Trentino, then still under Austrian rule.

Today the name of Cesare Battisti is famous and revered. He was the last of the martyrs to the cause of Italian independence and unity; fighting in the Italian ranks against Austria during the world war, although an Austrian subject and a deputy

[ 45 ]

to the Vienna parliament, he was taken prisoner and hanged by the minions of his country's oppressors.

Cesare Battisti and Benito Mussolini, imbued with a common spirit of lofty patriotism, had common ideals and aspirations. Their deeply Italian souls vibrated harmoniously in a spiritual unison that was later to burst forth in their common assertion of Italy's national rights.

Mussolini admired his friend's tenacious work, and Battisti held Mussolini's journalistic genius in high esteem. Mussolini received no remuneration for his editorial work; he lived on the 150 monthly crowns that he obtained as Secretary of the Trent Chamber of Labor. He sometimes eked out this meager salary by imparting French lessons to people who gave no exterior sign of being morons. He invariably refused to teach morons for any remuneration.

During his connection with "Il Popolo,"

Battisti gave Mussolini ample liberty to pursue his studies. Someone made an attempt to remind Mussolini that he was Secretary of the Chamber of Labor as well as editor, but he was properly snubbed. Mussolini, as a matter of fact, had little love for the Socialist organization of the Trentino, which had its headquarters in Vienna, and was very much in sympathy with the independent Czech Socialist movement. Consequently, Mussolini's activities in Trent were, for the most part, purely journalistic. The Clericals, whom he selected as his favorite opponents, still have rueful recollections of his brilliant editorials. When they nicknamed him "the bad boy" he wrote back:

"My dear Austrians, you must remember that you do not offend me in the least by calling me a bad boy, because Italy's bad boys are direct descendants of Balilla."

This thrust, reminding the pro-Austrian Clericals of the rout inflicted upon the Austrian troops in Genoa by the population led by a young boy, infuriated them beyond all measure.

But Mussolini's journalistic triumph was short-lived. His opponents, seizing the opportunity offered by a campaign that he was waging against them over the matter of Irredentism, in the course of which he had daringly asserted Italy's right to the unredeemed provinces, concluding with the prophetic statement: "Italy's border does not end at Ala!", had him arrested.

For a time he was kept in jail. Then he was released, but only on condition that he should leave Austrian territory and never set his foot back upon it.

# CHAPTER VII: MUSSOLINI THE ARTIST

PERSONAL EPISODES—MUSSOLINI'S FRIENDS—THE
UNFAILING FIDDLE—MUSIC AND POLITICS—
A MARRIED MAN AND HIS FIRST-BORN

A FRIEND of his relates:

I made Mussolini's acquaintance in Forlì, about twenty-five years ago, before he became editor of "Lotta di Classe."

At the Prati Café, where artists gathered, I met him and became his friend. He preferred small groups to large ones, and often he preferred solitude to both.

He did not refuse anyone's friendship, but he was very discriminating in his choice of friends. He had marked sympathies for my group, which was mostly made up of young and promising artists.

We spoke little about politics. Our conversations generally dealt with art: sculpture, poetry, and music. Benito was especially fond of music. In his moments of depression he always had recourse to his violin. From it he drew notes and harmonies in which the chords of his very soul seemed to vibrate.

We were all poor and obscure. We gathered at the café after supper; sometimes without supper. We were looked upon as eccentric characters, to say the least. Few knew of our privations and hardships, but despite appearances we all cherished secret hopes and ambitions. No one dreamt, at that time, that the man who sat with us would one day hold the destinies of a nation in the hollow of his hand. Yet only an inferior mind could fail to sense the fascination that emanated from Benito's personality.

His was a powerful, commanding figure; under his soft felt hat, we felt, there lurked a superior intellect; under his torn, threadbare coat beat a mighty heart, which was later to make all Italian hearts beat in unison with it. His short, black beard framed his pale face, which his great eyes illumined. His words were sharp and incisive.

He had little love for amusements or feasts. He disliked crowds, save in political gatherings, where he could electrify them with his fiery eloquence. He attended those gatherings frequently, running about the countryside every Sunday, and often on week days as well, to carry on his work of propaganda. His only diversion was the theatre, where he invariably sat in the balcony, refusing the orchestra seats which the kindly theatrical agent placed at his disposal. In the balcony, among the common herd, he felt that he could give full vent to his pent-up feelings, bursting into loud laughter as often as the production called for it. His noisy guffaws once availed him a reprimand from the policeman on duty, to whom he curtly replied that he came to the theatre to laugh, and that he would laugh as much as he pleased.

His violin had a great share in the formation of his character. Music is the best medium of expression for great minds, and Mussolini's favorite pieces were great symphonies and triumphal marches, the prelude, as it were, of his march on Rome.

One sunny afternoon, as I vainly tried to forget the pangs of hunger by walking about the streets, I came across Mussolini at the Prati Café. He was drinking a glass of milk. He invited me to sit down, probably understood from the expression on my face that I was hungry, and ordered a glass of milk for me.

"Drink," he said, "it will do you good."

I needed no second invitation. At one gulp the glass was emptied. He got up and paid for it with his last pennies, then said: "Come home with me; I'll let you hear a wonderful piece on the violin."

At that time he lived in a very modest apartment on a by-street. I was led into a scantily furnished room. He made me sit on the bed, drew out his violin and began to play Beethoven's Ninth Symphony. I am not a musician, but I can understand and appreciate music, and I must say that the execution moved me. Under the touch of his nervous, slender fingers the instrument seemed to throb and vibrate and the notes came forth clear and passionate, like a human voice. The exaltation of the musician communicated itself to me. His destiny seemed to grope for expression in those soft, deep chords.

Mussolini had few friends in Forlì at that time, because the Republicans constituted the predominant party and he was a Socialist. However, this did not prevent him from saying that the number of insanity and criminal cases had increased enormously since a stupid excuse for Socialism had taken the helm of the labor movement.

Kept under constant surveillance by the police and looked upon with suspicion by his own comrades because of his novel, aristocratic concept of Socialism, he found himself ill at ease among so many demagogues and lived in practical isolation. He earned his living by teaching French privately, but it was a scanty living indeed.

His father, who loved him dearly, often used to say to him:

"Benito, you are far too rash and outspoken."

To which he would boldly reply:

"Some day you will see what sort of a man your son is."

He was nearly always penniless. Once the two of us together could not manage to scrape up enough money to pay for a single drink. Yet one day, hearing that I was to deliver a lecture in a neighboring town, he came to me and asked me if I had any money. My reply was that I did not, but that it did not matter, since I would go on foot

MUSSOLINI'S FAMILY

Donna Rachele, his wife; Edda, his daughter; Bruno and Vittorio, his sons; Romano, another son, was born on September 27, 1927

and had friends in the town where I was going. Whereupon he produced a bicycle and ten lire and gave them to me with the remark:

"Better not place too much trust in friends."

He advised an organizer who spoke to the country people on market days to use the local dialect in order to make himself better understood. "Speak your own language, which is also that of your audience," were his pragmatic instructions on that occasion.

He was original in everything he did. One only had to see him walking about the streets of Forlì with his coolly superior air to realize that he entertained a good opinion of himself. He walked quickly, with an erect carriage, his eyes blazing and his hat askew. In winter he donned an old cloak that gave a further original touch to his figure.

He always seemed sulky, yet in his heart there lurked a spirit of exquisite kindness.

Mussolini's humor could nearly always be

determined by what he drank. He was almost a teetotaler, and generally ordered coffee or milk. But sometimes he would brusquely ask for wine, and then his friends knew that there was trouble in the air.

Very often, after we left the café, he would link his arm in mine and tramp the streets of the city with me until late at night.

Although his inclinations were aristocratic and solitary, he frequently felt the need of sincere friends. Being a man of discernment, he sought them among artists rather than among politicians.

During one of our walks under a wonderfully starry sky, Benito stopped at the Victor Emanuel gate. A cool breeze wafted a thousand perfumes to our nostrils. The trees swayed rhythmically in the wind.

"I wish I were a musician," he exclaimed, "so that I could pour into a single song, a single hymn, all the voices and movements of the universe!"

His eyes gleamed with a mystic light. I

wondered later on whether at that moment fate was weaving a glorious adventure for my restless comrade or whether he was weaving his fate. Perhaps the heroic, youthful spirit that was later to take him to the battlefield to give part of his red blood to the dear land that he unconsciously loved with a burning love was singing in his heart even then.

For even then, despite his Socialistic affiliations, Mussolini was proud to be an Italian. He was an avowed Irredentist as well. He often spoke to me with great satisfaction of an oratorical victory he had won in Trent while sustaining Italy's right to the unredeemed provinces. Even then he was opposed to demagogues and politicians, and in favor of true justice and his country's greatness.

After the agricultural strike of Predappio, his arrest was ordered. When the police appeared to arrest him he was reading.

"Please let me finish this chapter," he

said calmly, "Then I'll come right with you."

That evening I was in the Paggi Café when I heard that Mussolini would pass directly on his way to jail. My heart sank. A few minutes later he appeared, handcuffed like a common criminal, walking between two policemen and followed by a squadron of cavalry. His gait was quick and erect, as usual, and his proud, noble aspect inspired the curious with respect and filled the hearts of his friends and acquaintances with sorrow and impotent anger.

He was tried and convicted. I saw him several months later. He was in search of a cane which he had forgotten in the District Attorney's office. He loved that cane with the love that he might have had for an old and trusty friend. Fortunately it was recovered.

In Forli he lived with his father, who kept a sort of tavern outside the city gates. There Benito could be seen in the ill-lighted

barroom, seated at a table, with his head between his hands and his eyes intent on a
book, utterly oblivious of the noise around
him. He also spent a good deal of his time
in a miserable upstairs room, where he would
sit day-dreaming or reading works on sociol-
ogy, political science, languages, and literature.

It was in the tavern that he first met his
present wife. Their courtship was brief.
After his marriage, he left his father's house
and went to live in Venti Settembre Street,
with dame poverty in attendance.

When his daughter was born he bought a
little cradle with his last few lire and hap-
pily carried it home on his shoulder, amply
repaid for his financial sacrifice by his little
one's first smile.

But as his family grew, so did his needs.
His wife advised him to ask for an increase
in salary, blissfully unaware of the fact that
the salary only came at rare and uncertain
intervals. But he haughtily replied: "No,

never! I work for an ideal, not for a salary!"

When financial straits beset him most cruelly, he would take his violin, go up a wooden stairway to the loft and there vent his emotions upon the devoted instrument.

"Do you want to see something pretty?" he said to me one day. "Come to my house."

I curiously followed him. He led me to the sleeping baby's cradle and took up his violin.

"What are you doing?" I cried in alarm.

"I'm going to wake her up."

He began playing. A barbaric paean of joy came from the violin. The baby, of course, woke up and after smiling at her bearded papa, began to howl to the violin's accompaniment. This continued until Mrs. Mussolini appeared on the scene and sternly rebuked her husband and his innocent friend.

"You are a pair of senseless creatures!" was her parting shot as she took up the child in her arms in a vain effort to quiet her.

# CHAPTER VIII: MUSSOLINI THE REVOLUTIONIST

THE IDEALS OF SOCIALISM—FRIEND AND FOE ALIKE—
HAND-TO-HAND ENCOUNTERS—A WAR-LIKE PACIFIST

MUSSOLINI made many converts to the Socialist cause. A perpetual atmosphere of battle hovered about him. In Forlì he established a newspaper whose editorial policy had the vicious spitefulness of a machine-gun. This he entitled "Lotta di Classe" ("Class Struggle"), and made it the organ of the local Socialist party.

Then he gave himself over, body and soul, to the task of organizing the workers in Romagna. He wrote fiery, aggressively controversial articles, making himself numerous enemies, but arousing surprise and admiration even in the ranks of the opponents that he fought with the keen-bladed, chivalrous sword of his journalistic prose. His voice, inciting the masses to revolution, was heard everywhere throughout the province. He goaded the Republicans to fury, stormed against the Reformed Socialists and viciously lashed the right wing of his own labor organization, bringing about a state of restlessness and spiritual revolt in sunny Romagna.

In one of his articles he said:

"Today the Radical leaders who are at the head of the political and economic movement are either slaves to red tape or professional politicians. They do not hesitate to accept enormous salaries, their lectures are masterpieces of hypocrisy, they lack honesty, sincerity, culture and manhood. They openly say: 'To the devil with idealism!' and if some solitary figure arises to defend the true ideals of Socialism they look upon him as a lunatic. But we are proud to state that we still form part of this small army of lunatics!"

The tragedy of his life commenced at this period, during which he began to see through his comrades and hold them in contempt. He despised both men and money. "I repeat that I refuse any advance in salary!" he replied to the leaders of the Socialist party, who wanted to throw him a sop that would silence him. "One hundred twenty lire are enough for me. I have no desire to become one of the plutocrats of the Socialist organization!"

He equally refused to accept any remuneration for his editorial services. "Our problem is not to fill up a sheet of paper with words each week;" he wrote, "to us the paper is the emblem of the party; it is a banner; it is our very soul!"

The official Socialist party had become, in his opinion, "a putrefied corpse upon the stage of the Italian political comedy; or, to put it less drastically, a large drug-dispensing establishment on its way to bankruptcy."

But the ideals of Socialism were something entirely different: "Socialism is a rough, harsh thing, made up of opposition and violence; it is a war; and in war, woe to those who attempt to be merciful! It is something serious, terrible and sublime. Only by accepting this definition will Socialism become an accomplished fact, instead of a convenient means of livelihood for professional office-seekers. Socialism is not a thing for hucksters, demagogues or politicians; it is neither a romantic dream nor a sport. It is an individual and collective effort designed to lead to material and moral progress. It is perhaps the greatest drama that has ever urged human society on to span the gap that separates man the animal from man the human being with a bridge that will lead humanity from a state of struggle to a state of co-operation. Bread must come before the alphabet. Only through a long, arduous work of individual purification can the human element be created which is indispensable for the realization of this ideal."

Journalistic controversy was a sweet pastime indeed in that tranquil, idyllic province. From a single editorial published in a single opposing paper of the district, Mussolini, for his own amusement, once culled a complete stock of choice epithets, beginning with "thief," "swindler" and "crook" and winding up with "lunatic," "unscrupulous, hired tool," and "slimy reptile."

"Our life," he wrote in reply, "is an open book in which the only words that are to be read are 'study,' 'poverty,' and 'struggle.' Not even the shadow of the word 'corruption' appears therein. We feel strong because we feel pure, and because we have no friends and because we tend to restrict the circle of our acquaintances rather than to broaden it. We do not ask for popularity, following, or votes. We dare to speak the truth, frankly and brutally, even in the faces of our own followers."

Several attempts were made to kill him,

but then, as now, he seemed to bear a charmed life.

He had few sympathies for the Republicans. His lectures, which were most violent against the authorities that restricted the freedom of the workers and the bourgeoisie that exploited them, were not lacking in shafts directed toward the Republican party. In 1910 he insisted that at the First of May celebration the Socialists should not march in the Republican parade. He was wont to call Mazzini "Saint Joseph of Genoa." Consequently, the Republicans had no love for him.

One night, as he was returning from a lecture he had delivered at Villafranca, the Republicans planned to halt him and demand an explanation for certain editorial statements he had made. They went as far as to stop the stagecoach in which Mussolini was supposed to be coming back to Forlì, but instead of Mussolini they found four policemen in the coach, and swiftly took to their

RIDING AT VILLA TORLONIA

heels. Mussolini, by mere chance, had missed the stagecoach and came along a little later in a private coach.

The aversion between the two parties disappeared momentarily at the time of the war with Turkey, in opposing which both Republicans and Socialists joined forces.

When they tore up the car tracks outside the Garibaldi gate, Mussolini was arrested together with the two Republican leaders. They were put in the same cell and became fast friends.

Mussolini's defense at the trial became famous. He spoke for over two hours, outlining his revolutionary concept to the judges and proclaiming the necessity and, in certain cases, the sanctity of violence. In concluding, he said:

"If I were in your place, I would convict myself, because I am a rebel. If you acquit me, you will do me a favor; if you convict me, you will do me an honor."

When he had finished speaking his lawyer waived his right to speak, saying that he did not wish to spoil the splendid effect of Mussolini's speech. The presiding judge, turning to the jury, then said:

"Gentlemen of the jury, the man you see before you is no common criminal; he is a man of lofty intellect. Pass sentence upon him in accordance with your own lofty conception of humanity and justice."

The entire audience burst into applause for Mussolini and the judge, and as soon as the foreman of the jury read the verdict of acquittal, popular enthusiasm became unbounded and Mussolini was carried out in triumph.

He became the untiring organizer of the masses. In 1912, at the Socialist convention of Reggio Emilia, Benito Mussolini became an outstanding national figure. The Socialist party was languishing under the listless, unenergetic direction of the right wing leaders. Mussolini, in a brilliant speech, outlined his new doctrine and plan of campaign. The assembly was won over and the left wing triumphed. Bissolati, Podrecca, Bonomi, Cabrini and other right wing leaders were expelled from the party, while Mussolini was appointed editor in chief of the "Avanti!" the organ of the Italian Socialist party.

# CHAPTER IX: MUSSOLINI THE LEADER

AT THE PARTY'S HELM—A NATIONALISTIC RADICAL—
A HARD-FISTED PUGILIST

THE fiery editor of the "Avanti!" quickly imbued the depleted forces of the Reds with a new spirit. In a short time he put the paper on a paying basis and saved it from bankruptcy. In two years he increased the membership of his party from 50,000 to 150,000. His frankness and combative spirit won him popularity, while his burning oratory infused new faith and ardor into the discouraged hearts of the masses. His was not an easy battle. In addition to the capitalists, the young leader had to face the opposition of the Syndicalists and Anarchists. But he knew how to snatch victory from the very jaws of defeat, aided by the brilliant, compelling eloquence that spared neither friend nor foe.

He was a great admirer of Danton, and each year he commemorated the Paris Commune with a speech. One of these anniversaries fell on a rainy day. In comparison with the vast crowds that his lectures always drew, there was only a small number of Radicals gathered to listen to his words.

He waited over half an hour before ascending the platform. When he finally began speaking, with angry features and flashing eyes, he said to his limited audience:

"On a dawn that will forever remain famous in the history of the world, the revolutionists of the Commune launched their attack against the Bastille. They were not like the rabbits and lambs of the Italian Socialist party, who speak of social revolution and are afraid to face the rain!"

The party needed new energy and combative spirit. It needed, above all things, to be purged from the Democratic-Bourgeois infiltration of Freemasonry, which, recognizing Mussolini's worth, repeatedly made him seductive offers. But Freemasonry, to him, was the living symbol of the decay of the old ruling classes of Italy; it was "a catacomb of martyrs that had been transformed into a conclave of office-seekers." Nothing in Freemasonry appealed to him, neither its humanitarian, pacifistic, democratic, equalitarian doctrines, nor its adulterated internationalism, nor its fervid but hypocritical patriotism, nor its gross anti-clericalism, nor its puerile ritual, which aroused in him an almost physical repulsion.

At the convention of Ancona he had a resolution passed declaring Socialism and Freemasonry incompatible. Nine years later, in 1922, he was to declare the same incompatibility of Freemasonry with Fascism.

He was pitiless with the ambitious and ruthless with the vain. A Socialist who had literary yearnings asked Mussolini's permission to write a series of articles on class warfare. Mussolini, in return, asked him to write an article on "The Revolutionary Myth." The pseudo-writer, who had not fully understood the meaning of the topic, did his best and presented his article a few days later.

Mussolini read the manuscript with a stern face, in silence. The author bravely asked him:

"Well, what do you think of it?"

"I think you are the most egregious ass in the Socialist party," Mussolini coldly replied, "and I think you would do well to let literature severely alone."

He was frequently invited by Italian emigrants in France and Switzerland to hold lectures in those countries.

In Zurich, during the summer of 1913, he was speaking one day to a numerous audience in the local Italian Socialist Hall. His theme was suggestive: "The Contemporary Poets of the Revolution."

After exhaustively discussing the topic,

he quoted a few lines from well-known poems, dear to all Radical hearts.

Then, seizing his inspiration from the splendid summer twilight on Lake Zurich, he alluded, whether intentionally or accidentally no one knows, to the natural and artistic beauties of Italy. He did not call it "our country," for to speak of "our country" to those exiles would have been the same as to speak of a bad stepmother to the stepsons she had driven from home and abandoned to their fate. He simply recalled the sweetness of far-away memories, the peace of native towns, and the joys of home, which only an emigrant can fully appreciate. In so doing, he gradually aroused the heart-burning, soul-consuming homesickness of the exiles. Many an eyelash was wet with tears, many a throat was choked with sobs. Mussolini, although he perceived upon those weather-beaten faces the undefinable expression that arises from memory and longing, kept on speaking, insisting upon his topic, until from those pent-up breasts a powerful, uncontrollable cry escaped: "Long live Italy!"

It was one of the hottest days of a sultry summer season, and the thronging mass could scarcely breathe. Mussolini had already been speaking for an hour and a half. At one moment, thinking he detected a certain impatience in his audience, he asked: "Do you feel tired? Shall I stop?"

And that suffering, stifling mass of humanity, reeking with perspiration, shouted back as a single man: "No, no, go on, speak as long as you like!"

Mussolini spoke two and a half hours that day, and perhaps it was on that occasion that he realized that the glorification of one's native land, if inspired by true sincerity and love, has the power to sweep away all crowds, irrespective of party or political creed. Perhaps he learned that day that the masses, though oppressed and harassed by the daily struggle for bread, remain attached at heart

THE PEOPLE SUMMON MUSSOLINI TO THE BALCONY OF THE
CHIGI PALACE

to the distant memories of childhood, to the land where they were born and to the skies that first shone upon their dreams and hopes. Perhaps he understood that spirit is always predominant in man, and that spirit rises above the wretchedness and misery of the flesh to live its own life of beauty and grandeur.

Mussolini knew how to use his fists as well as his tongue. When he thought that an opponent deserved a physical lesson, neither obstacles of time and distance nor fear of arrest could deter him.

One day, while he was still editor of the "Avanti!" in Milan, he learned that the proprietor of a Geneva café had publicly slandered him. In spite of his former expulsion from Switzerland, he asked his friend De Falco, a political refugee, then editor of "L'Avvenire del Lavoratore" of Lugano, to accompany him to Geneva. With all due precautions, they arrived in that city. Mussolini lost no time. He immediately went to the café, which was crowded at that time of day, sought out the proprietor, and knocked him down.

This clamorous incident, of course, led to the discovery of his presence on Swiss soil. The police were ordered to arrest him at sight, but he managed to elude them. On his way back, while still in Switzerland, he stopped at Flamatt and lectured to the Italians for an hour; then he recrossed the border and returned to Milan, filled with the satisfaction of one who has accomplished a meritorious deed.

# PART THREE

# CHAPTER X: MUSSOLINI THE REBEL

AT the outbreak of the European war, Mussolini was one of the first and most strenuous advocates of Italy's absolute neutrality.

"To aid in circumscribing the war, since it is no longer possible to avoid it," he wrote in the "Avanti!" "is the noble task that Italy must accomplish. That is all that can be expected of us. The proletariat is on its guard. Our neutrality must be complete and absolute. We can be neither the henchmen nor the accomplices of Germany and Austria."

On October 10, 1914, however, realizing that the German Socialists were giving their

[ 81 ]

full-hearted support to the Kaiser, he wrote an article entitled: "From absolute to active neutrality," in which he openly maintained that Italy must prepare for war.

"Do you Socialists think," he said, "that the Republican or Socialist-Republican State of the future will fail to wage war if compelled to do so by internal or external historical necessities? Who assures you that a revolutionary government will not have to seek its inaugural baptism in war? Would you oppose a war that had for its purpose the saving of your revolution? To refuse to make a distinction between wars of various kinds, and to oppose all wars by the same methods, is to give evidence of downright stupidity."

Although he knew that this new attitude on his part would arouse hostility and unpopularity, he refused to compromise, and openly opposed the red mob that resisted Italy's intervention. Sincere, altruistic, endowed with the courage of his convictions, far-sighted, and bold to the point of rashness, he declared that the treason of four million German socialists and the alleged atrocities committed by the Germans in Belgium and France aroused in him a feeling of uncontrollable rebellion. In the face of the horrors of war, he awoke from the bright dream of universal peace and brotherhood that had once fired his heart, and while the Italian Socialists vainly apologized for their German comrades, and the latter marched through the streets of Berlin singing "Die Wacht am Rhein" and fraternizing with the militarists, Mussolini, in tones of thunder, denounced them both.

At the beginning of November, 1914, a general assembly of the Italian Socialist Party was held at Milan. The meeting lasted until three o'clock in the morning. Mussolini, without a tremor, appeared to face the judgment of his comrades and accusers.

When his turn came to speak, he left the small group of friends who had accompanied him and boldly walked down the aisle to the platform, between two rows of threatening fists raised in execration against him.

The red mob swayed, shouted, cursed. Mussolini was unperturbed. He ascended the platform and began to speak in a low tone, slowly and deliberately. He quickly overcame his first emotion, and his words became sharp, cutting, lashing. He, the culprit, turned upon his accusers in the guise of a judge and executioner:

". . . and I tell you, from this very moment, that I shall have no mercy for those who do not take an open stand in this tragic hour! I shall have no mercy for the reticent, the hypocrites, the cowards!"

While the mob clamored to tear him limb from limb, he raged at them and threatened them as though he were their absolute master. Alone against all, he never faltered.

In reply to the furious shouts of the fanatics, he fearlessly shouted back: "You hate me because you still love me!"

MUSSOLINI AT PLAY

Then he explained the motives that had led him to write his famous article. But that night even his stringent logic and fiery eloquence were powerless to calm the irreconcilables who clamored for his head. Then, seizing a water-tumbler that stood on the table before him, he crushed it in his nervous hand, and while the blood flowed down his arm raised in denunciation, he cried out to the Socialists who had accused him of treason:

"You have the power to expel me, but you cannot expel my ideas from my head! I can no longer remain deaf to the cry of distress that arises from war-torn Belgium and France, trampled upon by the only true traitors of the International, the German Socialists!"

A few days later, at the Bologna Convention, Mussolini was expelled from the party and removed from the editorial board of the "Avanti!"

# CHAPTER XI: THE APOSTLE OF WAR

HE left the Socialist party with only five lire in his pocket, but on the 15th of November he founded his own paper, "Il Popolo d'Italia."

"French gold!" cried out his enemies. But a jury composed of three Socialists and three neutrals, having examined the evidence, decided that Mussolini had collected the necessary funds among his friends and admirers and among advertisers who had paid in advance in order to help him.

"Il Popolo d'Italia" bore two mottoes: "*Whoever has iron has bread*—BLANQUI," and "*Revolution is an ideal supported by bayonets*—NAPOLEON." "Daring" was the

[ 87 ]

title of the first editorial, which ended with these words:

"As we resume our onward march, after a brief halt, it is to you, young men of Italy, hailing from farm and factory and college, to you, young both in years and in spirit, to you, members of the generation to which destiny has entrusted the making of history; it is to you that I launch my battle cry. It is a word that I should never have uttered under normal circumstances; it is a word that I utter aloud, proudly, defiantly, without reservations and with perfect confidence, as matters stand today; a fearful, fascinating word: War!"

Mussolini did not advocate war through a mistaken sense of sport or jingoism; he was firmly convinced that while on the one hand the Italian people had a moral obligation to go to the help of France and to free the unredeemed provinces, on the other hand Italy's full redemption called for a baptism of blood. Only war, to his mind, could arouse

the Italian people out of the shameful leth-
argy into which the democratic, liberal gov-
ernments of the past has allowed it to sink.

Mussolini perceived that the Italian
people vegetated rather than lived. "In vege-
tation," he said, "every healthy stimulus is
absent, and the painful but wholesome goad
of progress grows rusty. Man is trained to
imitate those cowardly species of nature
which feign death in order to leave the tragedy of peril to others. Every new conquest
of civilization is a peril and a tragedy, because, as Nietzsche said, the individual is
nothing. Or rather, he is a bridge, not a goal;
he must consider himself blessed because of
the day that is granted him to blaze the way
for future days. The creation of the future
is the great redeemer of life and comforter
of grief. The gods are dead; the day of the
superman approaches."

Mussolini called for a reversion to idealism, but to an idealism radically different
from that of the past generations.

"In order to understand this new idealism," he wrote, "we need a new, free spirit,
strengthened by war, solitude and peril; a
spirit that will liberate us from the doctrine
of the love of one's neighbor and the Chris-
tian desire to be passive, and restore active
purpose to the world and hope and ambition
to mankind."

He overflowed with self-confidence and
felt sure of victory. When he left the Socialist party many thought that his political
death-knell had rung, but six months later,
in May, 1915, his personality had become
one of the most outstanding in Italian political life. All of Europe, though torn, bleeding and struggling in the throes of a terrific
conflagration, watched him attentively.

In 1912, George Sorel, the great French
revolutionary philosopher, had written about
him:

"Our Mussolini is not an ordinary Socialist. It is my belief that some day we shall
see him at the head of a mighty legion, salut-

Mussolini on Board the Battleship "Conte di Cavour"

ing the Italian flag with his sword. He is a Fifteenth Century Italian, a Condottiero. He does not yet know it himself, but he is the only man of energy in Italy who can save the country from its government's fundamental weakness."

And as the silent, deadly struggle between the partisans of neutrality and the advocates of war came to a head, Mussolini stood forth more and more, like a bright beacon of hope, in the eyes of harassed, strife-rent Italy.

# CHAPTER XII: MUSSOLINI THE EDITOR

A LUXURIOUS NEWSPAPER OFFICE—HOW MUSSOLINI WORKS—WHAT HE THINKS OF JOURNALISM— BEAU SABREUR

HIS was an office of fantastic luxury, consisting of three large rooms in an old, tumbledown house in Paolo da Cannobio Street, Milan. The wall-paper fell in tatters, the desks were lame, and most of the chairs had no bottoms.

The editors were peculiar types, hailing from every part of Italy, but full of genius and enthusiasm, simplicity and generosity, and, above all, supreme faith in their ideal.

How they had first met Mussolini, no one knows. Even their names are now lost in obscurity. They were simply idealistic, hard-working young men, intensely interested in their work and their cause.

Mussolini had a sacred horror of documents and credentials. He required no school or birth certificates, no letters of recommendation. "If intelligence exists," he used to say, "it does not need to be duly filed away in the archives of Royal High Schools and Colleges." All he said to his assistants was: "Do something!" if they could do it, he took them on; otherwise, he did the work himself and escorted them to the door, bidding them a gentle but firm good-bye. In this way, he gathered about himself the most clever and pungent writers in Italy, as well as a chosen bodyguard of artists, musicians, orators, and organizers.

It was the youthful, gypsy-like soul of the new Italian generation that nightly invaded the three huge rooms in Paolo da Cannobio Street, shouting from desk to desk, scribbling, smoking one another's cigarettes, arguing vociferously, and composing, in the midst of din and pandemonium, the most lively, wide-awake and interesting daily in Italy.

There were signs up everywhere, on doors, walls and desks. Their mission was to govern the behavior of the editorial staff, the general public and the importunate outsiders who occasionally dropped in.

"Members of the staff are requested not to leave before arriving—that is, not to go until they have come," was the playful inscription on one of them.

"Whoever uses five words to say what could be said in one is capable of the darkest crimes," said another.

A third one, posted above Mussolini's door, bore the following legend: "He who enters does me honor; he who stays out gives me pleasure."

A fourth one, hung over a doorway from which the door was missing: "Please close the door."

And still another one, nailed to a desk:

[ 95 ]

"Whoever is unable to keep quiet while his colleague is working has no sense of pity for human misfortunes."

Such was the den of the enthusiastic, brilliant, child-like minds that were preparing Italy for Fascism and a new destiny.

Mussolini did not work extemporaneously. His cranial workshop was always active, but the work of preparation was invariably a mystery, even to those who knew him intimately.

When he got that far-away look in his eyes, when his strong-featured face acquired a scowl, and he went back to his private den and began ill-treating the papers on his desk in much the same fashion in which a nervous diner ill-treats his knife and fork, his co-workers knew that Mussolini was angrily hammering out his thoughts and imprinting his own indelible trade-mark upon them.

At such times his orders would snap out brusquely and irately, his gestures would become nervous and his glance ferocious.

"Boy, bring me some coffee. Don't let anybody come in here. I'll shoot the first man that enters."

"But I'll have to come in with the coffee, sir."

"Then I'll shoot you." The last with a reassuring laugh.

Then the door would close and complete silence would reign. Mussolini was at work.

On the bare wall behind him hung the great black flag of the "Arditi," Italy's war-time shock-troops, festively adorned with a white skull and a trench-knife. Upon his desk, between a barricade of books and a phalanx of manuscripts, lay a twenty-shot automatic, like an inverted question-mark. Further away, upon a volume of Carducci, rested a long, keen-edged hunting-knife, and near the ink-stand reposed another pistol, small and dainty like a lady's lap-dog. Stacked above manuscripts that will never see the light stood gleaming cartridge-cases, resembling the diabolic pipes of a warlike faun. In a corner of the den a small field-piece served as a stove.

Inside that formidable arsenal, silhouetted like a white phantom against the black background of the flag, Mussolini worked furiously, puffing like a steam-engine over his thoughts and ideas, hammering out new, incandescent phrases, cooking up food for the voracious linotypes.

Occasionally his co-workers outside could hear the labored breathing of "il Direttore" and the scratching of the pen upon paper, for all the world like the sound of a young tiger sharpening its claws. But his work was not impromptu, however much it might have seemed to be when he presented the finished product to his readers. His preparation was profound. Day after day, minute after minute, he prowled and sweated and cursed over his new creations, examining idea after idea, thought after thought, conversing fiercely with himself, discarding what he could not use, salvaging what could be of interest,

Mussolini Harangues the Mob

never resting until his labor was done and he was satisfied with the result.

He had no reference library or books of any kind in his den. Whatever he read became forever impressed upon the reference library of his brain. He never made notes or consulted a historical or political guide-book. No obstacle could ever stand in his way. So far as he was concerned, to think was to act. And he did his thinking everywhere, in railway coaches, in theatres during intermissions, even while conversing. He wrote at his desk, in his silent arsenal; he wrote in the midst of noisy friends, or while lying in a field hospital cot with a bleeding leg, or in a trench, during the intervals between bombardments, or at the table of a café. His home, his studio, his office were wherever he happened to be. He had no preferences. Like a soldier, he bivouacked wherever he happened to find himself, and resumed his march whenever he felt so inclined. He liked everybody but became attached to no one.

He did not recognize his own photographs, much less those of others.

He used to read his paper from cover to cover each day, scrutinizing it with the pleasure and eagerness with which an orchestra director listens to his musicians.

He loved his paper. He had an almost frantic affection for that insolent, bold child of his, and for the lively, restless, impetuous traits that it had inherited from him. At times, when he looked at the sheet which overflowed with life and aggressiveness, his mind would nearly succumb to an artist's temptation. "I'd almost like to destroy it!" he mysteriously confessed one day. When he was asked the reason why, he shrugged his shoulders, thought it over for a while, and finally remained silent.

He disliked professional newspapermen and journalists who failed to dramatize. His paper in consequence, was anything but academic. "Journalism," he said, "must be electric, alive, explosive!"

His own style was incisive and clear, in writing as well as in speaking. And he was, and is, a marvelous orator. His speeches have always had, to a superlative degree, the power of inflaming the masses. He usually speaks slowly, enunciating with care. His gesturing, sober for an Italian, is more than made up for by the mutable expression on his face. His usual gesture is simply a rhythmic, slow movement at his right hand, with thumb and forefinger held close together. But his face is a kaleidoscope of expression. When threatening, he lowers his head and clenches his massive jaws. When angry, he bends his head slightly backward, half closing his eyes. When promising, he leans forward toward his audience, softening his voice. He avoids empty phrases and invariably gives his words a vital content. He speaks extemporaneously, but with a precise, cutting logic. His speeches hold occasional outbursts and flights of fancy, but they can in no wise be construed as rhetorical or pompous. His personal magnetism is enormous, especially in the face of a crowd. He stands before his audience like a block of granite, filled with assurance, courage and energy. Around him all things seem fragile and transient, and men creatures of an inferior race.

His enemies and opponents have made the error of picturing to themselves a Mussolini, and consequently a Fascism, of their own creation. They have repeatedly stated that he has been bribed. According to the sum total of these accusations, he must have been bribed by everybody. He has been described as an adventurer hungry for honors and wealth, and fortified by a cynical, cruel ambition. Yet Mussolini has never loved wealth or feared poverty. It is indifferent to him whether he is clad in evening clothes or in an old threadbare suit, whether he dines in state in a luxurious restaurant or on a slice of bread and a cup of milk in the solitude of his room. In the office of "Il Popolo d'Italia," he would live for days on bread and salami, and he was known occasionally to sleep on the editorial desks. In the midst of duels and street encounters, he was always ready to face a new hostile attack, and hostile attacks were frequent in those days.

His reason for existence and his joy of living are in action. He is endowed with a volcanic brain and a will as keen and steely as a rapier. He never subscribes whole-heartedly to a formula or a doctrine, but stares ever-changing reality continually in the face in order to know and overcome it. He does not fear death, having faced it repeatedly without a quiver. Every day, when he was editor of "Il Popolo d'Italia," he received threatening letters from cowardly anonymous writers. He threw them into the waste-basket with supreme indifference, often not even deigning to glance at them. In spite of these daily death-threats, the attempts upon his life and the plottings of his opponents, he always appeared alone before the crowd that worshipped him because of his courage and ability.

An earnest advocate of speed, motion, and man's triumph over the elements, he has an almost frantic love for all kinds of sports. He is particularly fond of horseback riding and motoring. His driving is exceedingly rash. More than once he has broken through the barrier of a grade-crossing or the gate of a villa. He ventures on the brink of chasms and overcomes risky obstacles, almost as though he felt an urgent need of defying death.

One night the powerful motor-cars of the Milan police hotly pursued a speeding automobile on the Milan-Bologna road. People thought, on seeing the pursuit, that it was a criminal. But the criminal was only impatient Mussolini, bent on outdistancing his pursuers because he had an early morning appointment in a Bologna park for a duel with one of his political opponents. He was

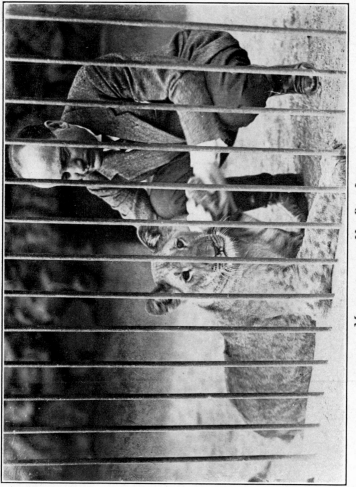

MUSSOLINI AND HIS PET LION

started the great conflagration prepared by Mussolini's indefatigable work.

Giolitti, the pro-German Premier who had used his influence to check the growing anti-German sentiment in Italy, was swept from power after a violent campaign conducted against him by "Il Popolo d'Italia." In vain he promised Italy territorial aggrandizement and the powerful friendship of the Central Powers in return for Italy's cowardly neutrality; in vain he appealed to the lowest, basest instincts of the masses, to their fear of war and death, to their desire for material gain; the true spirit of Italy, speaking through the poet and the orator, rejected all compromise and declared resolutely for war.

"As for me," wrote Mussolini, "I am firmly convinced that the safety of Italy requires that at least a few dozen Deputies be shot in the back as traitors. I honestly and sincerely believe that the Italian Parliament is the pestilential sore that poisons the life of the entire nation. We must remove it."

"War is the furnace in which the new revolutionary aristocracy is being cast. We participate in that war as radicals, revolutionists, and anticonstitutionalists, not as moderates, nationalists, and imperialists. Only a bullet will hush my voice."

On April 11 he was arrested in Rome, after a spirited meeting, and consigned to jail for a few days. Ten days later he fought a saber duel with Claudio Treves, a Socialist Deputy, and inflicted a slight wound on his opponent. Then followed a sequel of articles, tumults, defiances, threats, meetings and more duels.

Mussolini's endurance was miraculous. But now his powerful voice was echoed by another voice which came from France; that of Gabriele D'Annunzio, who, on May 5, 1915, the anniversary of Napoleon's death, spoke from Quarto, whence Garibaldi had set sail with his immortal thousand to free the South from the yoke of the Bourbons. The poet's sublime oration was the spark that war against the dying spirit of Italy in order to prepare Italy for the real war of the trenches and the mountain passes, on the Alps, on the sea and in the sky.

Mussolini founded his "Fasci of Revolutionary Action," and in January, 1915, these groups of strong, determined men numbered over five thousand adherents, scattered throughout all of Italy. At their first gathering, the founder addressed them with these words:

"I think that something new and wonderful will come out of these youthful maniples that have the courage of their heresy against established tradition. Today that something is war; tomorrow it may be revolution.

"Our intervention has a twofold purpose, national and international. It will contribute to the downfall of the Austro-Hungarian Empire; it will lead to a revolution in Germany, which in turn will spread to Russia; it will contribute, in short, to the cause of liberty and revolution throughout the world.

# CHAPTER XIII: MUSSOLINI THE PROPAGANDIST

FREE at last from Socialistic trammels, Mussolini devoted his newspaper to the support of the idealistic reasons that prompted Italy's intervention in favor of Belgium and France. It was a titanic task, because it meant the overthrow of the self-satisfied neutralism of a people accustomed for years to lead an easy-going, idle life, taking the course of least resistance, rather than looking forward to the accomplishment of an ideal crowned by the halo of self-sacrifice.

It also meant a war to the death against Giolitti, the bosom friend of Von Bülow, Germany's ambassador, and against the intrigues of a spineless diplomacy. It meant a

One may disagree with him, or even hate him, at a distance, but those who are near him cannot escape his subtle fascination. Even his enemies are forced to admire him and bow their heads under his lashing tongue and pen.

tired and nervous when he arrived, but in spite of that he managed to inflict a serious wound on his opponent at the twelfth encounter.

His predominant passion, however, is aviation. While training to gain a pilot's license he showed himself overbold. In one of his flights he fell and was hurt rather seriously, while his companions were killed, but this did not in the least dampen his enthusiasm for flying.

He is physically strong and morally courageous, self-confident, and conscious of his own superiority. Sometimes it seems that he is trying to test the courage of his followers by indulging in mad deeds of daring. When he undertakes a battle, he sacrifices everything, even his most sacred affections, in order to win it. Yet under the bronze mask of his Roman face a gentle courtesy and the ingenuousness of a child are often to be found lurking.

On May 15, he printed these few words in blood-red ink:

"The honor and the future of Italy are at stake. Our country faces the most tremendous dilemma in its history. The decision rests with the people. We want either war or revolution!"

And a few days later:

"Italian bayonets, the destiny of Europe, as well as that of Italy, rests upon your steel!"

On May 23, 1915, Antonio Salandra, who had succeeded Giolitti, obeying the will of the Italian people, declared war against Austria. The following day Mussolini wrote:

"Today the nation sounds its call to arms. Today there are no more parties; there is only the Italian nation. Today, as steel is about to clash with steel, a single cry bursts from our breasts: Long live Italy! Never as in this instant have we felt that the Fatherland exists, that it is an irrevocable factor in the destiny of mankind: never as in this instant have we felt that Italy is a historical, living, corporeal, immortal personality.

"To you, Mother Italy, we offer, without fear and without regret, our life and our death."

No Italian will ever be able to forget that bright springtime of 1915, when the clarion call of war sounded throughout the peninsula. From the snowy peaks of the Alps to the shores of sunny Sicily, from the wooded slopes of the Apennines to the storm-lashed crags of mysterious Sardinia, all was waving banners, marching regiments and songs of war. Everywhere the anthems of Mameli and Garibaldi resounded, as though Italy's sacred dead had arisen to march by the side of the living. The great Motherland, again girt with the sword of Scipio, was setting forth once more upon her tremendous historical mission, outlined in Virgil's immortal verse:

> *Tu regere imperio populos,*
> *Romane, memento.*

Italian hearts were aroused from their ancient slumber. From the august tombs of Arquà and Ravenna, from the austere sepulchers of Staglieno and Caprera, the spirits of Italy's great men seemed to shout back a reply and an encouragement to the shout of warlike enthusiasm that burst forth from the breasts of the living.

Whence had come that mysterious, elusive breath that had suddenly turned into a whirlwind, sweeping over the country and deciding it for war? Whence had come the popular urge that had metamorphosed the denizens of schools and offices, fields and factories, lecture-halls and laboratories, palaces and hovels into gray-green regiments that marched with measured tread and singing hearts toward the unjust frontier? How had a lazy, indifferent people suddenly arisen to demand war? How had simple peasants and humble workingmen, ignorant of the meaning of history, politics and philosophy, been suddenly won over by the energy of

Mussolini and the fascination of D'Annunzio, by the voices of the living and the dead?

The fact is that in the lives of nations, as in those of individuals, there are turning-points, decisive moments, when even the blind must see and the deaf must hear. As the fatal hour approaches, all must needs feel it; and when it finally strikes, all throw upon the funeral pyre of self-sacrifice every petty, selfish thought and ambition, because they feel that the great cause of social justice and right is at stake. At such times it is not only patriotism, but the love of humanity itself that spurs on nations and individuals. To defend humanity from slavery and oppression, all rise like the Theban phalanxes of old and march on to victory or death.

Italy, at the outbreak of a war unleashed by injustice and aggression, no longer felt bound to her unnatural allies of former years. Her intervention on the Allied side was the product of the outspoken will of the entire nation and the natural corollary of

Mussolini a Sentinel at the Front

Italian history, philosophy, literature and art. It was the victory of reason and idealism against fruitless materialism and empty positivism. Like all great spiritual revolts, it was not the result of the destructive philosophy that recognizes nothing beyond matter and profit, but the product of the powerful urge of an ideal, looking beyond immediate gain and spurring the nation to face all hardships and perils in order to bring about the triumph of justice.

When the brazen-voiced call of war sounded through the land, after the doubtful period during which the interventionists had faced both radicals and Giolitti's police in the streets and squares of Italy, the entire nation rose up in arms, ready to act and prepared for the final sacrifice.

# PART FOUR

# CHAPTER XIV: MUSSOLINI THE WARRIOR

REJECTED—ACCEPTED—IN THE TRENCHES—"I CAME HERE TO FIGHT, NOT TO WRITE!"—MUSSOLINI'S FORTY-TWO WOUNDS—MUSSOLINI MEETS THE KING

As soon as war was declared, Mussolini applied as a volunteer. His application was rejected, and he had to wait until his class was called to the colors. This did not occur until September 2. He left the direction of his paper in charge of his most trusted assistant, Giuseppe De Falco, and departed for the front. In his last editorial, addressed to his followers, he said:

"We, who are preparing to undergo the hardships and dangers of war, should like to feel that our backs are guarded. Keep your eyes open. Strike, if necessary, and strike hard. Don't give a minute's respite to the jackals and the traitors. Fight as we shall fight. That is the program I leave you."

He began his fighting career as a private in the Bersaglieri, Italy's renowned light infantry. He took part in several front line engagements. His colonel offered him a safe berth in the rear, with the mission of writing the history of his regiment. Mussolini replied: "I came here to fight, not to write!" And he stayed in the trenches.

"Because of his exemplary activity, his fine spirit and his serenity of mind; always first in every enterprise of labor or daring; contemptuous of peril, zealous and scrupulous in fulfilling his duty."

This high-sounding eulogy is only the motivation for his promotion to corporal. He never got beyond the rank of sergeant. His Socialistic past was against him. Once he was admitted to a speed training course for officers, but six days later the order came to send him back to the trenches, where he was needed. Neither surprised nor grieved, he returned to his fighting post.

During his few moments of leisure, he wrote a war diary, whose simple, analytic, realistic pages not only give a clear vision of war in all its fearful reality, but produce a deep and lasting impression in the mind of the reader, leaving a furrow of horror and pity which not even the passing years can erase.

In the trenches, face to face with imminent death, in the mud, beneath the rain, at the sight of soldiers who alternately prayed and cursed, the grandeur of the religion which radiates from Rome to the entire world first dawned upon him.

A few years later, when he spoke in Parliament on the Roman question, he astonished everyone by saying:

"There is a problem to which I wish to call the attention of the Party's representatives. That problem is the possibility of relations, not merely between us Fascists and the Catholic Party, but between Italy and the Vatican.

"From the age of 15 to 25 we have all drunk at the spring of Anti-Clericalism; we have all hated the cruel old Vatican she-wolf of which Carducci spoke, if I am not mistaken, in his ode to Ferrara; we have all heard about a 'sinister Pontiff,' as opposed to the august soothsayer of the truth, and about the 'black-haired woman of the Tiber' who pointed out a nameless heap of ruins to the pilgrim who ventured toward St. Peter's.

"But all these things, which are most brilliant in the field of literature, are anachronistic, to say the least, as far as we unprejudiced Fascists are concerned.

"I maintain that the Imperial Latin traditions of Rome are represented today by Catholicism. If, as Mommsen said thirty years ago, one cannot think of Rome without thinking of universality, I believe and affirm that the only universal idea in existence today comes from the Vatican.

"And, frankly speaking, I experience a feeling of regret whenever I hear of the founding of a new national church, because each national church means millions of people who no longer look to Rome and to Italy for spiritual guidance. Wherefore, I suggest that, provided the Vatican renounces its dreams of temporal power (and I think it is on the way to do so), Italy should place at the Vatican's disposal its schools, churches, hospitals and whatever else it may need.

"The development of Catholicism in the world, the increase of the four hundred million souls that converge toward Rome from all parts of the world, are matters of great interest and pride to us Italians. How can a millenary race, enriched and polluted by innumerable blends and invasions and scattered to the four corners of the globe, achieve full unity, unless it strengthens within itself the consciousness of its own universality and eternity? How can a nation be strong in adversity and great in victory if it gives itself up to the fallacious hedonism of selfish appetites and fails to translate its patriotism in terms of the absolute: God?

"The imperial strength of Catholic, universal Rome, of which Christ and St. Paul proclaimed themselves citizens, is a factor of our national unity which we cannot afford to disregard."

In the face of death, Mussolini was a constant source of comfort and encouragement to his comrades. He was always first where danger called. He was wounded several times, returning to the front each time as soon as his wounds had healed. His deeds of valor were repeatedly mentioned in the war bulletins of his regiment.

Meanwhile the hatred of the Socialists for their ex-comrade had by no means died out. A soldier in Mussolini's platoon received a letter from the Socialist leader of his village couched in the following terms:

"We have learned that you are fighting at the front with Mussolini, the notorious rene-

MUSSOLINI AT A RELIGIOUS SERVICE IN TRIPOLI

gade. You would do me a personal favor, not to mention the service you would render to the cause, if you could manage to shoot that traitor in the back."

But soldiers, under hostile fire, develop into loyal comrades. The Socialist showed the letter to Mussolini.

"People who stay at home," the latter remarked with a smile, "particularly if they are slackers, have very strange ideas."

One day the explosion of a trench-mortar inflicted forty-two wounds upon him, of which three were quite serious. While he was lying in the field-hospital at Ronchi, Sergeant Mussolini was visited by friends, generals and rulers.

"Hello, old boy!" exclaimed an old acquaintance on seeing him, "So these confounded 'minnies' minnied you!"

"You fire them off all the time, and they occasionally get even by firing you off," he laughed back.

He was not even unconscious when they

had picked him up. They say that he was gazing about him, in the midst of his dead and dying comrades, with the blood trickling down his face and his eyes just as fiery, wrathful and keen as though he had been addressing one of his favorite audiences. They pulled innumerable splinters out of him. His sufferings, in the course of the process, did not draw a single groan from his lips.

While he lay in a burning fever, with his eyes dilated and his teeth clenched, he was visited by the King. Victor Emanuel tried to say a few words of comfort, but Mussolini interrupted him:

"Reserve your kind words for the other wounded who are dying in this hospital, Your Majesty. I have to get well, because I still have to fight for my country."

When the King left his bedside, he was heard to murmur:

"That man will go very, very far!"

# CHAPTER XV: THE HIGH PRIEST OF PATRIOTISM

MUSSOLINI, the Socialist, had a passionate love for his country even then. One has to be far away from one's country, in a foreign land, in order really to appreciate and love it. The gods of the Fatherland often tramp the roads of exile. Frequently patriotism is felt more keenly by exiles than by those who quietly remain at home.

Mussolini had to spend several months in bed. He stoically underwent operations and physical suffering. When convalescing, he left the hospital on leave. Even his bitterest enemies grew silent on seeing him return home so pale and mangled and yet so impatient to get back to the front.

But he was honorably discharged because of physical disability. Whereupon, he gave himself up body and soul once more to his "Popolo d'Italia."

When he heard of the Caporetto disaster, he succumbed to a severe nervous breakdown. For seven days and seven nights he did not close his eyes, and his friends finally had to have recourse to morphine injections. In his fury against those responsible for the catastrophe, Mussolini decided to come to a final break with every remnant of Socialism, and his paper, which had hitherto borne the subtitle "Socialist Daily," now became the "Organ of the Fighters and Producers," uncompromisingly taking its stand against all movements, parties, and principles contrary to the nation's ideals.

He urged and encouraged the Italian youth to fight to the finish. Foreseeing the ultimate victory, he wrote in October 1918:

"A great battle is about to take place in the Venetian plain. In decisive clashes between nations, the roadways and battle-fields of history never change. The error of the Allies lies in their having allowed themselves to be bottled up in the trenches by the ponderous German spirit, unelastic and anti-dynamic because it lacks creative genius.

"A tactical warfare has been carried on everywhere, save perhaps on the Russian front. We have had a great deal of dilatory tactics and no maneuvering or strategy whatsoever. Decisive defeats are inflicted on the open plain, in pitched battles, not by laying siege to earthen fortresses. A break in the enemy's lines will result in a great battle that will drive the foe back not merely to his starting-point, but to the heart of his own country."

On November 2, he presented an extraordinary thesis:

"Will the masterpiece of our history and of world history take place on the banks of the Italian river after which it will be named? Will the new great clash between Nordics and Mediterraneans, between civilization and barbarism, take place in the valley of the Piave? Is it written in the book of fate that the defeat of Pan-Germanism, begun upon the banks of a river of France, is to end upon the banks of a river of Italy? We shall know within a few weeks, perhaps within a few days.

"In the meanwhile, let our hearts flutter with hope. The harassing questions of yesterday were: 'Shall we have enough coal? Shall we have enough bread? Shall we have enough firewood?' But today the citizens ask themselves: 'Shall we have enough iron, enough shells, enough bayonets?'

"We shall endure cold and hunger. They do not matter. Invasion is far worse than cold and hunger; it is humiliation. We will not endure that. We want to win! We must win! We shall win!"

Once more the morale, spirit and courage

of the Italians overcame the superior numbers and brute force of the enemy, this time decisively. Italy's gray-green hosts smashed the Austrian line at Vittorio Veneto and turned the Imperial defeat into an unparalleled rout, astounding even the Allies, who had little faith in Italian valor. The invaded provinces and the unredeemed lands speedily saw the Austrian hordes hard pressed in their flight by the victorious Italian army. Caporetto's disgrace had been more than effaced by the glorious, radiant triumph of Vittorio Veneto.

On November 4, 1918, Trent and Trieste were occupied. Austria sued for an armistice. After the immense holocaust of 700,000 Italian lives, sacrificed on the altar of the nation's unity, after four long years of silent suffering and uncomplaining grief, the war came to a victorious end.

Mussolini wrote:

"The great hour has come! In this hour of divine joy, tumultuous emotion suspends the beating of our hearts and causes a lump to rise in our throats. Our long and weary calvary, finally crowned by triumph, draws tears of joy from eyes that are tired from weeping. Let one immense shout resound from streets and squares, from the Alps to Sicily: Long live Italy!"

# CHAPTER XVI: THE NEW WAR FOR ITALY

A TRAGEDY OF ERRORS—THE GROWTH OF BOLSHEVISM
—THE RED TERROR

AFTER the armistice, many thought that Mussolini would sink back into obscurity. But such was not the case. The legions of the former shock-troops gathered about him, and he quickly became the leader of the war veterans, putting them on their guard against the wiles of the Socialistic foxes who were again beginning to raise their heads with impunity.

From the columns of his paper Mussolini exhorted the government and the nation to grant generous concessions to the soldiers who were coming back from the bloody trenches.

"We must not forget the hosts of those who are returning from the battlefields," he wrote. "We must give an internal, social interpretation to the war, recompense the masses that have defended the nation and bind them to the nation's future welfare."

But his words went unheeded by the government. The people, after an initial outburst of enthusiasm, were sinking back into their wonted apathy.

Mussolini's spirit rose in revolt:

"Enrico Toti, greatest of our war-heroes, your life and death are worth infinitely more than all of Italian Socialism! The innumerable rank and file of those who insisted upon war, knowing what war meant, who went to war, knowing that they went to their death, the thousands of brave men who form the proud constellation of Italian heroism, feel that the jackal pack is rummaging among their sacred bones, pawing the earth that was fertilized with their blood. But those glorious dead need have no fear! The hateful task is barely begun; it shall not be completed! We shall defend the dead, even at the cost of digging our trenches in the squares and streets of our cities!"

Only four months after the close of the war, he clearly perceived the necessity for Fascism: "We must again prepare weapons of iron and men of steel, and strike without mercy!"

He kept on writing violent articles against governmental sloth and indifference, and outlined a program of reforms and measures that the nation ought to have adopted in favor of all those who had risked their lives for their country.

But all the Allied nations, engaged in deplorable, disreputable squabbles, paid little or no attention to the soldiers who were returning home, worn out by the hardships of war.

Mussolini advocated a peace without reservations or compromises, a peace that would give Italy all that Italy deserved as a reward for her voluntary participation in the war. He was the only Italian journalist who, at the time, fearlessly supported D'Annunzio in his attacks against Wilson's Fourteen Points, for he already perceived that the doctrines of the American President were imbued with a pernicious sentimentalism that would wreak havoc with the Italian people. He saw that Wilson's doctrine, conceived and based upon an erroneous interpretation of European reality, was the capital foe of Italy's most vital aspirations and meant the nullification of the sacrifices that Italy had faced to bring about the realization of her ideals. The supine surrender of the Italian government to the orders of the Allied statesmen at the Versailles conference aroused Mussolini's most bitter aversion and contempt.

But Wilson's liberalism triumphed, aided and abetted by the spreading of a new, terrible spiritual disease, favored by the enforced unemployment and poverty which

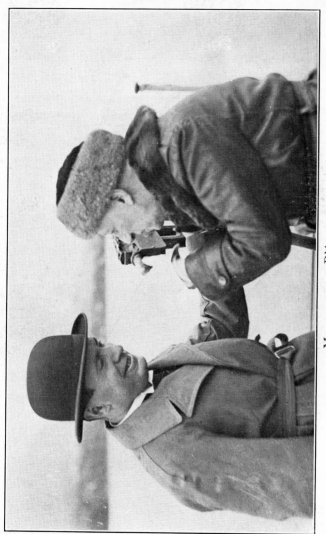

Mussolini and D'Annunzio

prevailed in the ranks of Italian labor immediately after the war.

Russia became the new ideal. The idealistic, undisciplined Italian soul, that had trustingly, enthusiastically followed Wilson, now, in disillusionment, turned to Lenin. A revolutionary madness burst out among the people and in the press. Even liberal, democratic newspapers began to hail and prophesy the advent of the Bolshevistic millenium. From the turbulent, starving, disappointed masses a single, fearful cry arose:

"Long live the revolution!"

The monarchy, the papacy, nationalism had become things of the past. There would be no more wars, consequently down with the army and the navy! Away from Trentino, Fiume, and the colonies!

Radical orators, openly and unmolested, urged the population to revolt, inciting the workers to slay, destroy and break the yoke of the bourgeoisie. Traitors and deserters walked about freely in the streets, thanks to

[ 137 ]

the amnesty granted them by Nitti, and the revolutionary press hailed them as heroes. Offensive publications and pictures against the King and the Army were distributed on the streets and posted on the walls.

When the victorious regiments decided to march in triumph through the streets of Rome, Nitti refused them permission to do so, reminding them of the threats of the Socialists and Communists, and ordered the triumphal arches that had already been erected to be destroyed.

In some cities the Radicals drove out the regularly constituted authorities, abolishing taxation, dispossessing the landowners, setting up their own marriage and divorce laws, and improvising a brutal Red Guard to replace the police. If a policeman, soldier or officer in uniform had the daring to board a train, the trainmen refused to start till he got off. The war-heroes, the war-maimed, from private to general, even the mothers, widows, sisters and sweethearts of the fallen, were publicly insulted in the streets, their medals torn from their breasts, their uniforms spat upon. Nor could the soldiers and officers defend themselves, because an order of the Minister of War forbade them to carry arms, and the Nitti Cabinet advised them to keep out of sight as much as possible and to wear civilian clothes whenever off duty. This humiliating decree could neither be forgiven nor forgotten by the military, and it undoubtedly served as a powerful incentive to many soldiers and officers to enlist secretly in the groups organized and directed by Mussolini. Even in Rome, the most peaceful city in Italy during that stormy period, people were killed like dogs on the streets for crying: "Long live Italy!"

Landowners and peasants were compelled to pay enormous contributions to the radical organizations, under penalty of seeing their crops destroyed. Italy was in a state of complete anarchy. Only a miracle could save it from revolution or chaos.

Yet all these excesses, murders and deeds of violence and intimidation were only the result of the sinister propaganda of a few hot-headed revolutionists who, backed by a small turbulent minority, imposed their will upon the great mass of the Italian population. They had two important factors in their favor, the government, which was thoroughly panic-stricken and did not dare oppose them in any way, and the powerful labor organization of the Reds.

This unhappy state of affairs was made more critical by the inertia of cabinets which did nothing to prevent the Reds from killing, burning, destroying and replacing the tricolor with the red flag. During this entire period, when energetic action would have been imperative, the government did nothing but submit to every demand made upon it by the Socialists and Communists.

Gradually the conviction began to take form in the minds of all law-abiding Italians that the state was powerless to defend itself or its citizens, and that the defense of the state and the individual against Red brigandage was a private, not a public enterprise. Deplorable as this state of mind may have been, it was the only way out of an impossible situation. The same thing would necessarily have taken place in any self-respecting nation where the government had stopped functioning and the forces of anarchy and revolution were oppressing the law-abiding majority of the community.

# CHAPTER XVII: THE BIRTH OF FASCISM

IN the midst of the darkness and terror
that attended the oncoming revolution, a
single gleam of light shone through the red
clouds that enveloped Italy. It radiated
from Mussolini and his "Popolo d'Italia."
Clearly perceiving the dismal abyss into
which the apostles of revolution were about
to plunge his country, he began, with sublime daring and at the risk of his life, to
preach the gospel of patriotism even more
fervently than he had done hitherto.

In March 1919 he summoned to Milan
his former army comrades and his political
sympathizers and founded his first "Fascio
di Combattimento," composed of 150 mem-

bers, young men filled with courage and a dauntless determination to stamp out at all costs the Bolshevik menace that was about to grip Italy.

The avowed purpose of the Fascio was "to function as an armed revolutionary group dedicated to the resurrection of the national ideal and to the destruction of the forces that were attempting to reduce the Italian people into a chaotic, amorphous mass, similar to the people of Russia."

At that time, this program seemed ridiculously impossible and doomed to certain failure. The Italian press completely ignored the foundation of the new revolutionary group. Only the "Popolo d'Italia" sustained its right to live and flourish, and Mussolini, in one of his editorials, prophesied to the remainder of the press:

"One day you will speak about Fascism! Yes, you will speak about it, and very much at length!"

When the radical press issued its threat:

[ 144 ]

"We shall erect our barricades in the streets!", Mussolini thundered back:

"Erect them if you dare! You will find us ready to blow them up underneath you!"

When the radicals cried out: "We shall begin our revolution," Mussolini replied:

"Go ahead! Begin it, if you are not bluffing!"

The humorous part of it was that it was Mussolini himself who was bluffing. If the radicals had had the courage, they could have brought a revolution to a successful completion at that time, for there was practically no one to resist them. But the disorderly, fanatical red hordes lacked a true leader. Nikolai Lenin knew it.

"Why have you lost Mussolini?" were the first words with which he greeted a delegation of Italian Socialists and labor leaders, who went to Russia in 1919 to present the red czar with the homage of Italy's reds, on the eve of their triumph. "You have made a great mistake. He was a resolute, energetic man, who would undoubtedly have led you to victory."

"Yes, I know," replied Trotzky to an Italian radical chieftain who was discussing Italy's real conditions with him, "they threw away Mussolini, their only trump card, the one man who could really have carried out a revolution for them."

Meanwhile Mussolini was gathering more and more adherents under the black flag of Fascism. His efforts were rewarded with un-hoped-for success. The sound element of the nation began to rally around him, beholding in him the leader of a movement that was to save Italy from annihilation.

Conscious of his ever-growing power, he stood erect and defiant in the midst of the Bolshevik whirlwind. Attended by his fol-lowers, his "darkest-hour Fascists," he went out into the streets, revolver in hand, dispers-ing the radicals and driving them back into their lairs.

At first, progress was slow. The Fascists,

Mᴜssᴏʟɪɴɪ Rᴇᴠɪᴇᴡɪɴɢ ᴛʜᴇ Cʀᴇᴡ ᴏꜰ ᴛʜᴇ Sᴜᴘᴇʀᴅʀᴇᴀᴅɴᴀᴜɢʜᴛ
"Cᴏɴᴛᴇ ᴅɪ Cᴀᴠᴏᴜʀ"

outnumbered ten to one, would come back decimated by death whenever they ventured out on a punitive raid. Then a brutal incident gave Fascism a sudden, tremendous impulse: the Socialist majority in the Municipal Council of Bologna deliberately planned and carried out, in the Town Hall itself, a massacre of the members of the Liberal and Fascist minority. Among those shot down in cold blood was Giulio Giordani, one of Italy's most famous war-heroes and an invalid. This savage murder of a defenseless cripple, who was loved and admired by all Italians because of his innumerable deeds of valor, created such a state of popular indignation that recruits began to flock by the thousands to the Fascist ranks. From that time, the Fascist movement gained impetus, acquiring new members and receiving the support and sympathy of the overwhelming majority of the Italian people.

It is undoubtedly difficult for Americans, born and brought up in a land where law and order are generally respected and enforced, to admit the possibility or necessity of a state within a state, of a military organization having the power to dispense justice outside of and above legal procedure, but this phenomenon has had a counterpart in practically all nations where the authority of the state was for a time weakened or non-existent. In America itself, the Ku Klux Klan of the reconstruction period and the Vigilantes of the Southwest employed methods similar to those of the Fascists, though their aims were different.

In September 1919 D'Annunzio seized Fiume. Mussolini approved of the Poet's exploit, which he looked upon as a defense of Italy's rights and a protest against the Treaty of Versailles. He gave D'Annunzio all possible material and moral support, and hailed him as a brother exponent of the spiritual revolt against anti-nationalistic degeneracy.

The whirlwind of Bolshevism gave no

sign of abating, but in every region of Italy the ranks of the Fascists grew, inspired by a powerful nationalistic sentiment and by the authority and magnetism of their leader.

Urged by his followers, Mussolini appeared as a candidate in the general elections of 1919. But the time was not yet ripe, and Bolshevism still enjoyed numerical superiority. He was soundly beaten. The Socialists, rejoicing over their victory, organized a monster mock-funeral, which filed for hours, in the murky night, through the streets of Milan, repeatedly passing under the windows of Mussolini's home, where his wife and children were anxiously waiting for news of their loved one. Mussolini, with a maniple of his followers, stood firm at his post in his newspaper office, ready to repel the expected attack of that multitude frenzied with hatred. To those who sang his "Requiescat" he replied with a defiance that sounded like the death-knell of haughty despair. But despite their overwhelming numbers, they knew him and his followers too well to attempt direct physical violence that night.

The news of his defeat was hailed with joy by radicals of all shades. But the Leader of the Fascists still remained as a stumbling-block in their path.

One day a laborer from Genoa appeared in the office of "Il Popolo d'Italia," and asked to speak to the editor on a private matter. The suspicion of the staff was aroused by his mysterious behavior, and Mussolini was warned. Nevertheless he decided to receive his strange visitor in his private office.

The laborer had a revolver in his pocket, but when he found himself face to face with the man he had vowed to kill, he changed his mind. Before the piercing eye and calm scrutiny of the man who had faced a thousand storms, the Genoese laborer confessed the true purpose of his visit and surrendered his weapon to Mussolini.

Mussolini took him out to dinner and paid his fare back to Genoa.

Mussolini Visits One of Italy's Newest Ocean Greyhounds

A few days after his electoral defeat, Mussolini was calmly seated in his office, facing one of his assistants. Beneath his window a red parade was filing by with shouts of: "Death to the bourgeoisie! Death to Mussolini! Long live Russia!"

In front of Mussolini, on his desk, was a large glass of milk which he occasionally stirred with a teaspoon, and within reach of his hand lay his inseparable revolver. From the street came the ever more menacing howls of the red mob, the thunderous voices of the police who guarded the building, the rattle of musket-butts on the cobble-stones. Mussolini, calmly and dispassionately stirring his milk, remarked to his assistant:

"They shout and yell and threaten and make a deuce of a noise, but after all, they are a pack of cowards. Don't think for a minute that they would have the courage to come up here. They know that in order to get me they would first have to face my revolver, and they know that I could kill at least two of them before they could touch me; and in all of Milan there are no two of them who are brave enough to face certain death. So, I drink my milk."

Premier Nitti was overjoyed to hear of Mussolini's defeat, and had the office of "Il Popolo d'Italia" searched no less than four times in one day.

Only the truly faithful continued to remain around Mussolini now that the icy blast of failure seemed to have blown upon him. "That was an unfortunate attempt!" said one fair-weather friend. "The people are tired of wars and patriots!" hinted another. "Don't worry!" il Duce replied calmly, "Have faith and patience! Within two years, I promise you a wonderful victory!"

One misty day in November a police officer entered the office. "Professor," he said with a sarcastic smile, "the Police Commissioner would like to speak to you."

"Tell the Police Commissioner that I have

nothing to say to him," Mussolini replied evenly.

The officer had no warrant. "Very well," he said, and departed. A few hours later he came back, this time with a warrant. Mussolini said:

"I have defended Italy in the streets, in the trenches, in newspapers, with my pen and with my sword. I have nothing on my conscience. However, if my arrest can help you to restore order, I am ready to accompany you."

Thanks to the energetic protest of some friendly Deputies, he spent only one day in prison.

It was on this occasion that the "Avanti!" jokingly reported that Mussolini's putrefied corpse had been found in the river Naviglio.

# CHAPTER XVIII: THE BLACK SHIRTS

THE EPIC OF FIUME—THE SONG OF YOUTH—
THE FASCIST LEGIONS

FORTUNATELY for Mussolini and his movement, D'Annunzio maintained his occupation of Fiume, which became the rallying-cry of Fascist gatherings and the watchword of the Fascist doctrine.

It was at that time that the Italians in America sent Mussolini, who was looked upon as D'Annunzio's right-hand man, over two million lire for the sacred cause of Fiume. In Fiume's name, Fascist groups were organized in every district of Italy. The black shirt, worn by the shock-troops during the war, and now a part of the uniform of D'Annunzio's legionaries, became the symbol of the new patriotism.

Fiume finally fell under the guns of Giolitti's regulars, but Fascism, stronger than ever before, was now powerful enough to make a determined, nation-wide stand against Bolshevism, which at the beginning of 1920 held in its serpent-like coils the chief industrial centers of Italy, especially in Piedmont and Lombardy.

Mussolini organized a military staff, composed of former army officers. Fascism became, in every sense of the word, a government within a government, with Mussolini at the head of an armed, well-trained militia, ready for attack or defense.

The Bolsheviks, with Giolitti's acquiescence, proclaimed the triumph of the proletarian revolution in Italy and seized the factories. Mussolini retaliated by giving his Fascists the order to attack.

The Black Shirts, replacing the powerless police forces of the government, enveloped the Bolsheviks in a whirlwind attack, drove them from the factories, burned down their newspaper plants, destroyed their halls and co-operatives, waged incessant, strenuous war against them. Under the furious impact of the Fascist offensive, the entire red movement crumpled and collapsed.

At the 1921 elections, when Mussolini again appeared as a candidate, he won overwhelming victories in two cities, Milan and Ferrara. The former gave him 190,000 votes, while the latter, after thirty years of undisputed Socialist sway, sent its women to lay the red flags at the feet of the victor, that he might pass over them in triumph.

"What will Mussolini do in Parliament?" now asked his foes, insinuating that the fascination of political power could corrupt the most adamantine character.

But Mussolini passed unscathed through the temptations of parliamentarism, as he had passed unscathed through the bullets of his foes.

His new parliamentary duties did not keep him from attending personally to the organization of the Black Shirts whom he loved and in whom he beheld Italy's only hope of salvation.

The Fascist legions that he created were composed of the flower of Italian youth. As they marched past their Leader with legionary tread, saluting him with the ancient Roman salute, it was easy to perceive that their hearts were firm, their bodies sound and their minds determined. Their clear gaze betokened a spirit of absolute obedience and faith in their commander, and their erect, austere bearing evinced their consciousness of the importance of their mission. Their features were those of the virile, handsome, daring heroes of classic times, similar to the Athenian youth that Phidias immortalized in the bas-reliefs of the Parthenon, with their thoughtful serenity and super-human spirit of self-sacrifice.

Like avenging angels, they proceeded from town to town on their terrible mission of social justice, singing the song of youth that their precursors, the black-shirted shock-troops of war days, had sung on their trench raids. The original hymn of the shock-troops contained bloodthirsty allusions to the trench-knife and hand-grenade that formed the sole equipment of the raiding parties; the Fascist version, on the other hand, was modified to suit the new circumstances that had arisen since the war. A fairly accurate translation of it was rendered by Francis Medhurst in the April 23, 1927 issue of "The Literary Digest":

## I

Up, my comrades, in your thousands!
   March to meet the future bright,
Rank on rank, serene and fearless,
   Swift to battle for the right!
Triumphs now the great ideal
   Bought with blood from sea to sea;
Brothers all throughout our country
   In Italian aims are we.

# MUSSOLINI

## *Refrain*

Youth! Ah, youth! Thou lovely thing!
Time of beauty's blossoming!
Fascism doth surety bring
Of our people's liberty.

## II

Lo! No longer is our nation
    Spurned and humbled in this hour.
To a new life she has wakened
    Rich in glory, great with power.
Lift on high the torch resplendent
    That shall light us on our way!
Industry and peace shall win us
    Perfect freedom in our day.

## *Refrain*

## III

Through long vigils in the trenches
    Streamed the bullets' leaden spray
All about the flag we followed
    In the thickest of the fray.

Victory shall crown that banner
  If like men we play the game.
'Tis our Italy that wills it;
  Let us conquer in her name!
         *Refrain*
         IV

Rouse ye, too, O sons of labor!
  Your redemption is at hand.
Heed not those who would destroy you;
  Keep the Red flame from our land.
Tear the masks from all the traitors
  Who would forge a chain for toil.
To the stocks with them for planning
  Asian plots on Latin soil!
         *Refrain*

Two years after its official inception, Fascism already appeared to Mussolini himself as something "extraordinarily distant, veiled by the mists of time and legend."

"Fascism arose," he said, "out of a deep, perennial need of our Aryan, Mediterranean race, which at a certain moment felt

[ 161 ]

menaced in its very existence. I myself, who am looked upon as the father of this movement, sometimes feel that it has already broken the modest bounds that I originally had assigned it. It has no ready-made program, to be brought to completion in the year 2,000 or thereabouts; it builds up the structure of its will and its work day by day."

Mussolini's habit of saluting with his hand led to the re-establishment of the old Roman salute, executed with the right hand instead of the left, in military posture, with head erect. The names and formations of ancient Rome were also resurrected; legions, cohorts, centuries, maniples, decurions, centurions, consuls, the division of soldiers into principes and triarii, the swift, orderly march by threes. All this was done not through a tedious process of archaeological research, but with the automatic spontaneity of an atavic instinct. The mechanically understood principle of false equality, which

Rejoicing Parade of Fascist Workmen After an Unsuccessful Attempt on Mussolini's Life

had ruined the well-meaning efforts of Socialism, was replaced in Fascism, not by the symbol of an impossible quality, but by that of a deeply felt brotherhood: the black shirt, which was a direct descendant of Garibaldi's red shirt and had received its baptism of fire in the war, was equal for all ranks, from the highest to the lowest. It was to the red shirt as the silent discipline of modern fighters is to the impetuous, individualistic, romantic daring of 1848; the allegory of an equal courage, but of a more austere spirit of self-sacrifice.

Banners and mottoes sprang up: the lictorial ax and the eagle of ancient times, the trench-knife and war-club of more recent origin; the shout "A noi," used by the shock-troops as they went over the top, the military-slang "Me ne frego!" consecrated by D'Annunzio, and the "Eja, eja, alalà!," the ancient war-cry of the Greeks, also revived by D'Annunzio for the use of his flying squadron in the raid over Vienna.

[ 163 ]

"Fascism is a typically Italian product, just as Bolshevism is typically Russian," Mussolini once said. "Neither of the two can be transplanted or live outside of its native land."

A by-product of the war, the Black Shirts reflected in their behavior the fundamental military virtues of courage and loyalty, daring and discipline, initiative and responsibility. They also reflected the shortcomings of their warlike training, which in civilian life often lead to serious consequences: impulsiveness, inclination to violence and a scanty regard for human life. Light-footed and light-hearted, because of their popular origin, they tended to disregard the serious and sad part of life. They were the incarnation of agility, vitality and ardor, the incarnation of youth on the march toward a new dawn.

# PART FIVE

# CHAPTER XIX: THE SAVING OF ITALY

CASTOR OIL AND CLUB—ANARCHY AND GUERRILLA WAR-
FARE—FASCISM'S FIVE THOUSAND DEAD—HOW
A GENERAL STRIKE CAME TO NAUGHT

IN the midst of stark tragedy the Fascists frequently found amusement in the use
of original and highly persuasive forms of
punishment, such as the complete shaving
off of the flowing locks and beards of the
Bolsheviks or the forceful injection of a
strong dose of castor oil into the most outstanding opponents of Fascism.

These methods were also employed with
great success in combating immorality, crime
and drunkenness. In Alessandria, criminals
were warned that any of their number
caught in the act would be clubbed in such
a way that he would become a fit candidate

for the hospital rather than for prison. Alessandrian crime ceased as by enchantment.

The Fascists of Adria, tired of the perennial drunkenness of certain of the inhabitants, affixed manifestoes on the walls in which they said:

"Anyone found in the streets in a state of intoxication will receive half a liter of castor oil. Every wine-shop keeper found guilty of serving alcoholic beverages to people who are already drunk, or to minors, will be given the same dose. Furthermore, a large bottle of castor oil must be exposed in a prominent place in all wineshops and cafés, to serve as a reminder to eventual transgressors and to eliminate delay in the punishment of those who disobey these regulations. We are not joking."

A humorous episode occurred in Arona, where the Socialists had decided to stay away from the ballot-boxes on election day in order to mislead the public as to their possible strength. The Fascists, on learning of this decision, covered the walls with announce-ments which said:

"Whoever refrains from voting on elec-tion day must be sick. All those who are sick need a physic. Whoever does not vote will receive a regulation dose of castor oil."

The Arona Socialists, without a single ex-ception, appeared at the ballot-boxes. Strange to relate, the Fascists won by an overwhelm-ing majority.

In 1921 Mussolini wrote:

"The Nineteenth Century is now on trial. In industry, democratic government has proved a dismal failure wherever tried. Even in Russia they have been forced to institute factory dictators. Politics will soon have to follow the example of industry."

In the early part of 1922 he was even more explicit:

"The democratic war par excellence, the war that was to lead nations and social classes to the 'immortal' principles of democracy, has come at the very beginning of an anti-

democratic century. 'Everybody' is the typ-
ical slogan of democracy, the slogan that
filled up the Nineteenth Century. It is now
time to say: 'The few and the elect.' A return to classicism is at hand. Revolution lies
in reaction. It is a revolution of salvation,
because it saves Europe from the miserable
doom that would have befallen it if democracy had continued to reign supreme. This
century is not the continuation, but the anti-
thesis of the last."

But the few and the elect could not con-
vert an entire nation to their ideas simply
by making use of theoretical and philosophical arguments.

"However much one may deplore violence," said Mussolini, "it is evident that in
order to force our ideas into some brains we
have to use a club. Punitive raids must always have the character of a just and law-
ful reprisal. We are not waging war against
a school of thought, a philosophical system
or an esthetic idea. Violence must be gen-

erous, chivalric and surgical. There is to be no petty individual violence, of the type that is often worse than useless. Our violence must be the great, austere, inexorable violence of decisive moments. After all, whenever strong contrasts of interests or ideas arise in history, it is always strength that has the final word."

Until August 1922, Fascism was an insurrection of the patriotic part of the population against the violence of the radical element. The government had proved feeble and incapable of coping with the situation and protecting the rights of its citizens. The country's laws were overthrown. The Parliament and Senate were bodies without authority or prestige. There were only two real powers striving for the mastery of Italy, Radicalism and Fascism. Every day bloody encounters occurred, with heavy casualties on both sides. For over two years a practical state of civil war had existed, intense, desperate and saturated with hatred. But even the authorities were now convinced that the salvation and redemption of Italy lay in Fascism.

In August, 1922, the situation suddenly changed. The radicals had declared a general strike on a futile pretext. In reality, they wanted to bring matters to a show-down by paralyzing the nation's life and thus bringing the government and the Fascists to their knees.

The Fascists immediately mobilized their forces to face the new economic menace that threatened to plunge the country into anarchy. Michele Bianchi, Secretary General of the Fasci, before 20,000 Fascists assembled at Sarzana, read an ultimatum addressed to the government and couched in the following terms:

"If within the next forty-eight hours the state takes no measures to control the situation, the Fascists will do what the government proves incapable of doing."

For forty-eight hours, the Fascists limited

Mussolini in 1922

themselves to averting the paralysis that threatened to crush the life out of the nation's economic and social structure. They ran the trains, landed cargoes, supplied the cities and towns with food, and operated the public services. At the end of the period assigned, seeing that the government had made no attempt to intervene, the Fascists took the law into their own hands. Punitive raids on a large scale were made into workmen's sections. The strikers were given their choice between returning to their jobs and going to the hospital. The vast majority of the workers returned to their jobs. The strike came to a sudden and inglorious close, and the nation breathed once more.

This ungentle, but highly efficient method produced surprising results. The middle classes, now thoroughly aroused from the supine tolerance with which they had undergone Bolshevism, rallied around Mussolini and hailed him as the savior of his country. Victorious Fascism became the new religion of Italy. The streets that had once echoed with the cries: "Long live Wilson!" and "Long live Lenin!" now resounded with the praises of a single, native idol: "Long live Mussolini!"

The failure of the general strike marked the end of Bolshevism in Italy. The triumphant whirlwind of Fascism swept over the country, urging it on to its new, lofty destiny.

In less than two and a half years, over 5,000 Fascist youths had been sacrificed to the nation's redemption. Daring, strong, afire with faith and courage, they had fallen in city streets and country lanes, the victims of fratricidal steel and bullets. The inscription dedicated to the Italian Unknown Soldier may well be applied to them:

"The worthy son of a proud race and a millenary civilization, he resisted inflexibly in the most contested trenches, displayed his courage in the most bloody battles, and fell fighting, without any other reward than that of hoping in the victory and triumph of Italy."

Today every Fascist tomb is an altar, a symbol of faith and virtue, of courage and self-sacrifice, of the nation itself, a bright beacon that will forever shed its light on coming generations to mark out for them their everlasting goal, the greatness and glory of Italy. Kneeling at the Fascist sepulchers, the Italian people today commemorate not only the youths who sacrificed themselves for the sake of their country, but also the heroes and martyrs who fell to create the nation that the Fascist dead were to preserve.

# CHAPTER XX: A BLOODLESS REVOLUTION

DURING the months of August, September, and October 1922, there were so many applications for membership in the Fascist organization that by the first of November the Squadristi, members of the militant section of Fascism, amounted to half a million, the ordinary members to one million, and the workingmen enrolled in the Fascist labor organizations to two and a half million.

At the Naples convention, held on October 24, Mussolini, the Leader of this vast army, finally realized that he held at his absolute disposal a force that would enable him to overcome all obstacles.

[ 177 ]

"Either the government is handed over to us peaceably," he said to the Fascist delegates convened in the San Carlo Theatre, "or we shall take it over ourselves, marching upon Rome and engaging in a death-struggle with the miserable politicians now in power."

Over his black shirt, together with the insignia of commander-in-chief, he wore that day for the first time a sash with the colors of Rome.

"What are we doing here in Naples? It's raining here; but the sun is shining in Rome!" shouted one of his lieutenants after his departure. And the convention adjourned in orderly tumult, with a shout that was like a battle-cry, repeatedly drummed out in steady rhythm:

"Ro-ma, Ro-ma, Du-ce, Du-ce, a Ro-ma, a Ro-ma!"

On October 26, Mussolini went back to his newspaper in Milan. Like the good general that he was, he had felt the pulse of his troops and was fully satisfied. In his mind, the die was already cast. He now began to formulate his plan of action in its political and military phases, conceiving and elaborating it unhesitatingly and with iron determination.

He began by forming a Quadrumvirate, composed of Michele Bianchi, Secretary General of the Fasci, Dr. Balbo, commander-in-chief of the military forces, DeVecchi, a soldier and a politician, and Gen. De Bono, the former commander of the Grappa Army Corps. Each of the four was assigned his own special work. Grandi, a former Deputy who had been excluded from Parliament because of his youth, was appointed chief of staff for the Quadrumvirate, with the added mission of carrying out all purely political details.

De Vecchi and Grandi immediately left for Rome. It was their mission to inform the King of the events that were about to take place and to compel Premier Facta to

[ 179 ]

resign. Facta was reluctant, but after pressure had been brought to bear upon him by Salandra and Orlando he finally resigned with his entire Cabinet on Friday night, October 27.

The first objective of the political plan had been attained, but time pressed. Code telegrams kept the wires burning between Rome and Perugia, where the Fascist military staff had set up its headquarters, while Mussolini, from Milan, directed every move. His apparent absence from the capital was part of his plan, for he needed unlimited freedom of action, desperate action, if the need should arise.

The King was already aware of the general situation. It was now necessary to inform him as to the immediate purposes and aims of the Fascists. This, too, Grandi and De Vecchi accomplished successfully, thanks to the co-operation of influential sympathizers. Italy's first Soldier had a clear concept of the destinies of his Kingdom; his enlightened mind had grasped the significance of the momentous events in progress, and he had already chosen his course.

Grandi and De Vecchi, thinking their mission accomplished, left that same night for Perugia. But at nine o'clock the following morning De Vecchi received an urgent telephone call from Rome, requesting him to return at once. The King wished to see him. The situation was becoming more serious than had at first been expected, and there was not a minute to lose. The danger of a clash between the regular army and the Fascist militia had arisen, and the military authorities were preparing a plan of defense for Rome.

De Vecchi and Grandi left for the capital at once. They arrived at two in the afternoon. Immediately after their arrival, they were joined by Ciano, Mussolini's personal emissary from Milan. Disquieting rumors were circulating. Everywhere throughout the country the Fascists had begun to seize public buildings and military barracks, in furtherance of the plan of local action which formed part of the general plan. In a few cities the police and military had attempted to resist. In Cremona there had been casualties on both sides. The Fascist envoys felt an icy clutch at their hearts. At that very moment, the newsboys began to shout an extra: Facta's resigning Cabinet had proclaimed martial law!

A fleeting spasm of agony passed over the frowning faces of the two Fascists. At that instant, they beheld a frightful vision of civil war and revolution in all their bloody efficiency. But they were men of action. Their intentions were at once made manifest. "In that case, we shall go on to the bitter end! God save Italy!"

But Ciano reassured them. In the midst of the distressing reports just received, he had remained calm. He had private information to the effect that the King, inspired by God for the welfare of the nation, had refused to sign the decree of martial law presented to him by Facta.

The three Fascists wept with joy. Their nervous tension found wholesome outlet in tears. Fratricidal war and bloody revolution were avoided. No blood would flow. With light hearts and a cheery smile, the Fascist envoys now set about the work of collaborating in the bloodless plan of occupation.

Salandra informed them that he had been requested by the King to form a new Cabinet, and led them into the presence of the monarch.

"I want the Italians to know," said Victor Emanuel to De Vecchi, "that I have refused to sign the decree of martial law." And after a pause he added, with a weary smile upon his face furrowed by the cares of state, "But perhaps within one week the Italians will have forgotten!"

"No, Your Majesty!" replied De Vecchi emphatically, "They will not forget! We shall remind them!"

In the evening of that same day the Fascists were officially requested by Salandra to participate in the formation of his Cabinet. But Salandra knew, even as he made his request, what the outcome would be.

Mussolini's reply from Milan was brusque and concise:

"I refuse to participate in any Cabinet of which I am not the head. The Fascist victory must be complete."

Whereupon Salandra also resigned. The moment was exceedingly critical. Swiftness and energy were needed as never before. De Vecchi and Grandi realized full well that the slightest incident might cause the entire edifice that they had built up with so much pain and labor to crumple like a house of cards. One hundred thousand Fascists, thronging along the highways of the ancient Roman legions, were clamoring for admittance at the gates of Rome. Every effort had to be made to prevent their entrance into the city before the political negotiations for the

MUSSOLINI RECEIVED BY THE KING AFTER THE MARCH ON ROME

creation of a Mussolini cabinet came to a head. Only when the situation had become stable could the Fascist irregular army be permitted to enter. Meanwhile, time pressed.

The Fascist legions were well-disciplined, but impatient. Some of them were bivouacking in the icy rain, entirely ignorant of what was going on. Even their leaders knew nothing. Both men and officers were in a state of harassing uncertainty. Was it civil war, or merely a demonstrative action that awaited them? Were they to enter the capital as brothers or as foes?

De Vecchi and Grandi implored the King to summon Mussolini to Rome without further delay. And the King, on Sunday morning, spoke the word that put an end to all uncertainty.

The Leader of Fascism, sitting cool and iron-willed in his office at Milan, refused to share the impatience of his followers. He insisted upon documentary evidence of the King's summons.

"I shall come by aeroplane, if necessary, but not until I receive the King's telegram," he replied to the urgent requests of his friends that he come at once.

The telegram reached him a few hours later. He left for the capital at once.

Outside the gates, he passed his Black Shirts in review. After so many days of anxiety, fear and joy, the devoted followers of Fascism finally entered Rome, with their Leader at their head.

When Mussolini appeared before the King, wearing the black shirt of his movement and with a revolver slung over his shoulder, he spoke these memorable words:

"I beg Your Majesty to forgive me for appearing in your presence in uniform. I have just come from a bloodless battle which had to be fought. I bring back to Your Majesty the Italy of Vittorio Veneto, consecrated by a new victory. I am Your Majesty's devoted servant."

[ 186 ]

Half an hour later, from the government palace, Mussolini, Italy's new Premier, spoke to the Fascists and the people:

"From this day you have not only a Cabinet, but a government."

# CHAPTER XXI: ON THE ROAD TO ROME

THE MARCHING HOSTS——AN ARMY'S PRIVATIONS——
FLOWERS AND BULLETS——THE ETERNAL CITY

WHILE this anxious, nerve-racking political battle was in progress, the black-shirted cohorts of Fascism had been relentlessly closing in on the capital. Let us follow them in their epoch-making march along the historic highways of the Roman legions, from the beginning of their mobilization to their triumphal entry into the Eternal City.

The selection of Perugia as headquarters of the Fascist general staff had not been haphazard. Geographically, Perugia was the fulcrum toward which the three attacking columns, coming respectively from northern

Italy, the Adriatic seaboard and the Tyrrhenian coast, would have to converge.

Perugia fell easily into the hands of the Fascist vanguard. On Friday, three mysterious visitors arrived at the Hotel Rufani; they were Michele Bianchi, General De Bono and Italo Balbo. The only missing member of the Quadrumvirate was De Vecchi, who had gone to Rome with Grandi. In the immediate vicinities of Perugia, 3,000 Fascists, under Consul Graziani, lay in concealment.

At 11 o'clock that night the 3,000 Fascists stealthily began their advance. By midnight they were at the city gates. At the same hour, the Prefect, who was in bed, received a surprising call from a Fascist delegation, which gave him half an hour's time to make arrangements for the peaceful occupation of the city. Otherwise. . . But that was superfluous. The Prefect, after making the arrangements, was escorted back to

his sleeping quarters, where he vainly tried to regain his lost slumber.

A few minutes sufficed for the occupation of the prefecture, the railway station, the post office and all other public buildings. A printing press was requisitioned and began at once to turn out manifestoes to the population, announcing that the buildings were in the hands of the "Fascist Government" and that the same thing was occurring at the same time in other Italian cities.

But Rome was still in the hands of the old regime, which shortly afterwards made its existence known in a curious way. At eight o'clock in the morning, the telephone bell in the prefecture rang. Michele Bianchi, who had been sitting up all night, answered.

"Hello!"

"Hello!"

"This is Mr. Ferraris, Premier Facta's secretary, speaking. Whom am I speaking with?"

"Mr. Arcelli."

"Arcelli? I don't think I know you."

"Very well, then, I'll tell you the truth. This is Michele Bianchi."

"Ah! I understand!"

"So much the better!"

And the conversation proceeded in a bitter-sweet fashion, with Bianchi courteously but imperatively requesting Ferraris to inform Facta that the Fascists had seized Perugia, and warning the "fallen government" not to do anything rash and to avoid bloodshed between the Fascists and the regulars, adding that the Quadrumvirate would hold the "fallen government" responsible for all unpleasant incidents that might occur.

Meanwhile, the Fascist army was pouring into Perugia. The military organization of the forces had been carefully worked out, with the troops divided into legions according to the provinces from which they came, and with consuls and inspectors in charge of each division. An army of occupation of

,000 men was held in readiness to
to Rome, with an immediate reserve
000 of Foligno, under the command
General Zamboni, the hero of Mount Pa-
subio, and an ultimate reserve from southern
Italy that should have advanced from the
South along the Appian Way, had the need
for such action arisen.

The greatest preoccupation of the leaders
was to prevent all conflicts between their
men and the regulars. Soldiers and policemen, according to the strict orders issued,
were to be sacred, for they were to form the
bulwark of the coming Fascist government.
Clashes must be avoided at all costs, and the
consuls were held personally responsible.
Mussolini, who had planned every detail,
had appointed regular army generals with
a reputation for bravery to command each
column. They were to expose their breasts,
covered with the emblems of heroism, to
the regulars, in case of conflict. If necessary,
they were to be the first to sacrifice them-

selves. But all were ready for sacrif[...]
historic motto, "Rome or death!"[...]
all lips.

During the night from the 27th to t[...]
28th, the general order to advance was given,
and the Fascist legions began their historic
march.

General Fara's column, 12,000 strong,
left Florence for Monterotondo, where it
was to join Igliori's forces. A single passen-
ger train was in the station, with no pas-
sengers except the Fascists. A noblewoman,
bound for Rome, expressed her annoyance
at this state of affairs to a Fascist aide-de-
camp, a former captain of the shock troops.
The latter put all of his Fascist propaganda
into play and finally convinced the Countess
that if she really wanted to go to Rome, the
only way to do so was with the Fascist troops.
His offer was gratefully accepted, and the
Countess, joining the Fascists, became the
mascot of the Fara and Igliori divisions, with
which she shared the hardships of the voy-

Mᴜssᴏʟɪɴɪ Hᴀɪʟs ᴛʜᴇ Bʟᴀᴄᴋ Sʜɪʀᴛs ᴏɴ ᴛʜᴇ Aɴɴɪᴠᴇʀsᴀʀʏ
ᴏғ ᴛʜᴇ Mᴀʀᴄʜ ᴏɴ Rᴏᴍᴇ

age and later entered Rome in triumph through Porta Pia.

The two divisions proceeded by train to Orte, but three kilometers from the station they found the tracks torn up and obstructions placed in their way. The track was promptly repaired, but some time was lost.

The men had brought only one day's rations with them, but the population flocked to their rescue. Bread, meat, fruit, vegetables and wine were showered upon the marching columns by the inhabitants of the towns through which they passed. Where food had to be requisitioned, receipts were left which were afterwards converted into cash.

From Orte the Fascists reached Monterotondo by train. Here they were greeted by the welcome news that all danger of civil war was past. Mussolini had been summoned by the King. By a forced march along the Nomentana highway, Fara and Igliori's 20,-000 men reached Rome on the afternoon of the following day.

The Bottai division was the only one that entered Rome amid the din of musketry. Bottai had personally directed the mobilization of the Fascists from the Abruzzi and the Marche, who had come down from their mountain homes wearing their picturesque native costumes and armed for the most part with hunting-rifles. Theirs was the strongest and most characteristic legion, consisting, as it did, of the veterans of the Pinerolo Brigade, the heroes of the Isonzo front.

They bivouacked at Villa D'Este, in perfect comfort, with their wants fraternally attended to by the friendly inhabitants. They were impatient to reach Rome, which they held at their mercy by reason of the fact that they had seized the capital's central power-house and water-main. Bottai kept them at bay all day Sunday. On Monday it became necessary to draw closer to the capital, and the Fascists left amid the hails of the population, which showered them with flowers, palm leaves and laurel branches.

As they approached the capital they were besieged by peasants who brought them water, eggs and milk. But at the very gates of Rome they were met by a regular army general, who requested them to change their course in order to avoid passing through San Lorenzo, Rome's Communist suburb. Bottai, conscious of the fact that Igliori and Fara had already preceded him into the capital, curtly refused, and marched up to the gates. Here he made a brief speech to his followers, reminding them that Mussolini was already in power, that they were entering as sustainers of law and order and that they must avoid all unpleasant incidents and even endure insults in silence, if necessary.

The column marched on through the silent gates. The streets of the suburb were deserted. The windows were tightly shut and barred, as if to betoken the hostility of the inmates. Half way through the suburb a window was suddenly opened; but the hand that appeared dropped flowers instead of bombs. There was some applause and cheering on the part of the Fascists as they marched past the friendly window. But the suburb retained its hostile appearance. It seemed to be keeping some unpleasant surprise hidden up its sleeve.

Suddenly the crash of rifle shots rang out. "Halt!" The head of the column stopped abruptly. But it was a sporadic case. The bulk of the division marched on, leaving only the rearguard to keep up its action against the hostile windows. Ten minutes later the battle was over. The column marched on in peace to the Altar of the Fatherland.

Night was falling. The commanders ordered their troops to stand at attention, but the legionaries paid no heed. They had all fallen to their knees before the Tomb of the Unknown Soldier while the Abruzzians of the Teramo cohort laid upon the altar a gigantic wreath that had been religiously carried during the entire march.

The most proletarian of the columns, so to speak, and the one that passed through the severest hardships, was commanded, by an irony of fate, by a Tuscan patrician of illustrious blood, Marquis Dino Perrone-Compagni, whose blasé, aristocratic demeanor remained unruffled in the midst of all the vicissitudes that befell his column. From Tuscany the division, 20,000 strong, came by train to Santa Marinella, a tiny bathing resort, where public buildings were few and small and the palatial villas of the Roman aristocracy hermetically sealed for the winter. Private property had to be respected, for the legionaries were not bandits. And so thousands of men passed a night and a day in the rain, under the dripping trees. But not a complaint escaped their lips, though their feet sank deep in the mud and their military capes were soaked through and through. In fact, they even blessed the rain, because when they had first arrived, parched with thirst,

[ 199 ]

they had found no drinking water, and their attempts to boil and filter the sea water had met with dismal failure.

Hunger also fell to their lot. Food was scarce. Groups of five men were to be seen gathered about a decurion who divided a loaf of bread and the contents of a tin of meat into five rations. Some had nothing but a piece of army biscuit to gnaw upon. Yet they sang and joked.

They had better luck when they reached Civitavecchia, whose friendly inhabitants came to their aid with linen, shoes and overcoats, while the regular military authorities, despite the possibility of a conflict in the immediate future, distributed food to the famished men.

Civitavecchia, however, was still slightly infected with radicalism. In one house the Fascists unearthed about eighty armed Communists. Perrone gave the order to shoot them. But first he decided to harangue them in the public square. In the course of his

IL DUCE

THE FOUNDER AND LEADER OF FASCISM
(From a Painting)

oration, he lost his vindictiveness, waxed emotional, and finally told his victims that he would spare their lives and set them free if they would promise to reform and amend their evil ways. Some of the Communists burst into tears at this unprecedented generosity: others cried out: "Long live Italy! We have been deceived!" The population cheered, and the ex-Communists dispersed to their homes.

Rome was only a few hours away. The march was resumed at once, and the division reached the capital without further incidents.

Perrone and Captain Vitali, a war-hero, went to pay their respects to Mussolini, who had just returned from the Quirinal. Mussolini, seeing the gold medal on Vitali's breast, embraced and kissed him repeatedly.

The troops were in a frenzy of joy. At last they were in Rome, amid the festive greetings of the population. Many of them had never seen the capital before. Some had pawned their wives' earrings or sold part of their winter stock of wool to spend a few days in Rome at their own expense.

But Mussolini's stern orders were necessarily pitiless. All must go home immediately after the parade: every Fascist must leave Rome. A few hotheads, a few criminals who might have slipped by chance into the Fascist ranks, might do irreparable damage to the cause. It was hard to leave Rome, beautiful, divine Rome, after traversing its streets and squares in military formation, seeing it only as through a dreamy mist, amid the thunder of applause and showers of roses, with the vision of a gray-haired man at the windows of the Quirinal, surrounded by generals and admirals, smiling at his faithful, devoted Fascist soldiers as they filed past.

But orders were orders! Away from Rome! Now the Fascist hosts owed a double duty of obedience, as Fascists and as citizens. Mussolini was at the helm!

# PART SIX

# CHAPTER XXII: A NATION'S HERO

TODAY Mussolini is Italy's Premier. Seated at his desk in the Chigi Palace, he works for the material and moral reconstruction of his country, attended by the love of the Italian people, who see in him the embodiment of all their aspirations, the man whom Italy vainly sought for many years, when powerful, enlightened minds were needed to steer the ship of state.

Today Mussolini is the Leader of the Fascist party. Around him still flock the brave and bold, the men whose sacred ideal and heartfelt religion is their country's welfare.

He is still young and full of vigor.

Ever since his accession to power, he has

shown that he possesses a sound, firm concept of politics, together with all the requisites of a high-grade executive. Unlike Utopian idealists who set out to alter the course of history in accordance with their own preconceived theories, Mussolini has not attempted to create the new without taking into consideration the old. Like every true man of action, he has shown himself to be at the same time a revolutionist and a conservative.

He has rendered homage to the King and the Army. He has shown that he possesses the inhibitions necessary for refraining from becoming intoxicated with power. He uses Fascism for the ends that a new historical reality points out to him.

"Our work begins today; we have destroyed; now we must reconstruct," he said to his followers, while issuing orders to his leaders to the effect that discipline and respect of life and property must be strictly, inexorably enforced.

As the victorious leader of an irregular

militia, he said to the Army: "I want no honors. The army must neither applaud nor disapprove. It must simply and always obey."

He said to the Prefects: "All government officials, from the highest to the lowest, must faithfully perform their duty. I shall set the example."

He wired D'Annunzio: "We shall be sufficiently intelligent and tactful not to misuse our victory."

He sent the following message to all Italian Embassies and Legations abroad: "I expect a new and broader love of country to transpire from the actions of all of you."

To the American Secretary of State he sent this telegram: "On assuming the government at the request of His Majesty the King, I send you my most cordial greetings, trusting that the friendly economic and spiritual co-operation that has always existed between our respective countries will continue. This is all the more a pleasure to me because the Italian people look to the American nation with perfect confidence that it will be able to understand and appreciate the efforts put forth by the Italian nation to achieve the common victory."

To the Italians in America he sent this message: "On the anniversary of our victory, it gives me great pleasure to send a message of good will to the Italians who reside in North America. Just as the young men who came back victorious from the trenches united into a powerful organization, similar to the conquering legions of Rome, and succeeded in giving the nation a position worthy of the victory they had won, so are you also asked to form, in the name of Italy, a spiritual union that will give evidence of your strength and display the virtues of the Italian people even outside their own boundaries. Thus united, you will co-operate more efficiently not only for your own prosperity, but also for that of the noble Nation that gives you hospitality and of which you are an important constituent factor. Italy

Mussolini Arriving in Tripoli (Africa) with General Del Bono, Governor of the Italian Dominions

has issued from the war with an increased sense of her own power and dignity. This same consciousness must make you proud of your Italian blood and cause you to honor the name of Italy wherever you may be. Long live Italy! Long live the United States!"

Discipline and work are the mainstays of Mussolini's internal policy. Peace and conciliation synthetize his foreign program.

What does Italy's Premier desire from the Allied nations? Simply the realization that in Europe, between the Alps and the three seas, there is a nation called Italy, with a territory slightly over half that of Texas, on which forty million people live and multiply: that while other nations of Europe are on the way to extinction, Italy's population increases at the rate of half a million a year; that Italy is no longer "the land of the dead," as Lamartine defined her, nor, in the words of Metternich, "a geographical expression," but a living, pulsating, growing, powerful organization that the Powers can no longer afford to disregard.

Mussolini wants more respect for the land of Dante and Machiavelli, Da Vinci and Michelangelo, Galileo and Columbus, Verdi and Garibaldi, Saint Francis and Savonarola, Marconi and D'Annunzio, the heroes of the Piave and Vittorio Veneto. He wants the voice of the nation that was a vital factor in the world war to be heard; he wants its strength and power to be recognized; he wants the Cinderella of the nations to awaken and receive a worthy place among the nations of the earth.

Mussolini does not want a territorial empire for Italy, but he does want a spiritual empire. He wants the Mediterranean for the Mediterranean nations. His foreign policy has been based and will be based on the principle of justice and fairness to all, Italy included.

Fascism today is at the peak of its power. Since the march on Rome, Italy has made wonderful progress and achieved surprising results; the morale of the Italian people has risen again, order has been restored, work intensified in every field and factory; the battle for the defense of the lira begun and won; the government put on a paying basis; the struggle for the intensification of agriculture brought to a successful completion; a great organization of syndicates of workers, employers, professional men and artists created, with the result that class war has come to an end and strikes have disappeared; the colonial issues have been closed; the Fiume question done away with; treaties of friendship and compulsory arbitration signed with many nations of the old and the new world; the question of the war debts to Great Britain and America settled; the campaign for the Lictorial loan successfully carried out, and the corporative plan of the Fascist State realized by means of the Labor Charter.

After this comparatively short, but strenuous period of Fascist domination, Mussolini is able to state with justifiable pride:

"We have the merit of having changed the government into a living organism, duly functioning in the national society, and replacing a red-tape, inefficient government that allowed itself to be attacked and insulted in a sort of absurd duel in which the opposition was sacred and intangible and had all rights, while the government only possessed the privilege of constituting a comfortable, indulgent target for the attacks of its opponents. I declare that this is an absolutely suicidal theory, and if the doctrine of liberalism is embodied in this theory, I am strongly anti-liberal."

Notwithstanding the profound changes that have taken place in Italy within the last few years, Mussolini repeats:

"We have accomplished nothing as yet; at least, nothing new. We still have a constitution that is like a twelve-year-old girl's dress worn by a florid woman of twenty. In

Mussolini Surrounded by the Flower of Italy's Naval and Political Leaders on Board the "Conte di Cavour"

1848, when that constitution was promulgated, there was no Italy; Piedmont was a strong state, but it was small and in the progress of formation; there was no press, there were no means of communication, there was no industry, there were no large cities. The little dress is short and tight, threadbare and full of holes; yet people cry out: 'It must not be touched!' Why not? If it no longer fits, it must be changed."

When he speaks of the future generations, his eyes kindle with the clear, cold light of his unbending will.

"Twenty thousand leaders, teachers, engineers, bankers and manufacturers; five thousand army officers; three thousand magistrates; ten thousand public officials; all first-class, specialized men, imbued with organic technicism to the marrow; that is what Italy needs; that is what I am preparing for her. From forty to fifty thousand men who will function like clockwork, marking the hours of Italy's greatness, specialized for the good of the nation, and constituting a directing class. We have enough, and more than enough, politicians. Great technical aristocracies have to be reared and trained; they are not born ready-made."

The term "dictator" does not exactly describe Mussolini, for there are many kinds of dictatorship. Nor does it suffice to say that he is Premier, Minister of Foreign Affairs, of War, of the Navy and of Aviation. He is also at the head of the syndical organization, and this is perhaps what is of the most importance.

The present Italian Constitution sufficed to invest him, through royal appointment, with the command of the land, naval and air forces, and with the direction of internal and foreign affairs, but only the new syndical organization could give him complete control over the nation's economic and social life.

Fascism, which in its initial stage was simply a dictatorship of force, partly supported by the collaboration of the vanquished parties, has recently assumed a specific character, which justifies its uncompromising attitude and takes the undoubtedly original form of a dictatorship of organization.

At no time was a government ever based upon a broader foundation. The creation of the Department of Corporations is a new starting-point in Italian political life. The fact that it has boldly faced and successfully solved one of the most difficult problems of contemporary society will ever be one of the chief merits of the Fascist dictatorship. Only through Fascism have all the producing classes of Italy become integral parts of the State, with economic representation replacing the political representation of the democratic-liberal doctrine.

"We have buried the old, democratic, liberal, agnostic, paralytic Italian state," said Mussolini in one of his speeches, "the state which, in homage to what it chose to call its 'immortal' principles, permitted class warfare to be turned into a social catastrophe for

the entire nation. We have replaced this anti-
quated concept of the state with the co-opera-
tive Fascist state, which unites, harmonizes
and controls the interests of all classes, ex-
tending equal recognition and protection to
all. It is perfectly absurd to accuse the Fascist
regime of being against the people or the
laboring classes. The truth is that only since
1922 can it be said that the people themselves really rule this nation. Previous to
that time, we had a government of cliques,
factions and parasites.

"Today we impose our discipline upon the
nation, and the people accept it. Why? Because they feel, know, and understand that
this discipline does not arise from my own
personal whims, but from the long-felt needs
of the country. Sometimes I must act like a
surgeon, because operations are at times indispensable, but when the patient recovers he
clasps the surgeon's hand and kisses the in-
struments that have restored him to health."

The foes of the regime bewail the lack of

liberty. "If there is any man in Italy who has no liberty, that man is myself," replies Mussolini, "but I accept my servitude as the highest reward that can be offered me. The word 'liberty' has been replaced by the words 'order,' 'hierarchy' and 'discipline,' which are today the only words that exert a real life-and-death fascination upon the fierce, restless, bold masses of our younger generations."

When he writes that "Fascism has trampled, and if necessary will trample again upon the more or less decomposed corpse of the goddess Liberty," he explains his meaning by further stating that he denies liberty "if liberty consists in the right to perturb the life of the nation and show visible contempt for the symbols of patriotism and religion."

A dictator does not and cannot compromise. Mussolini stands today for a policy that is absolutely, theoretically and practically uncompromising. "All power to all Fascism," is his motto. "Today Fascism is a party, an army, a corporation. It must yet become something more: a mode of life. There must be Italians of Fascism with unmistakable characteristics, just as there have been Italians of the Renaissance and Italians of the Roman Empire. Only by creating a mode of life shall we be enabled to write indelible pages in history as well as in the daily press.

"This mode of life is made up of courage, boldness, love of danger, repugnance for sedentary life and pacifism, frankness, freedom from diplomatic and political intrigue, the pride of being Italians, the discipline of work and respect for authority. De Bernardi, Nobile and De Pinedo are samples of this new type of Italian, whose slogan is, 'to make of one's whole life one's whole masterpiece.' "

"To live dangerously," is Mussolini's favorite motto, of which he wants himself to be the living, fearless, instructive exponent. After the latest attempt upon his life, he ordered his Fascisti:

[ 218 ]

"IL DUCE" IN UNIFORM OF HONORARY CORPORAL OF THE
FASCIST MILITIA

"If I advance, follow me; if I retreat, kill me; if I fall, avenge me!"

Such is the fascinating character of this dictator and his power of attraction and dominion over forty million Italians.

Fascism is an aristocratic ideal, a spiritual renewal without which no material, economic or political reconstruction would have been possible.

The Italian manhood, composed of the mature generations that learned to temper their former skepticism in sorrow and the younger ones that sought their inspiration at the fount of war, has seen the rebirth of the old Roman ideals.

The former exile and conspirator, the faithful depositary of the sacrifice of millions of the dead and the daring standard-bearer of the will of millions of the living, is finally at the helm of the State. While the Rome of the money-changers writhes in agony under the lash of his condemnation, he lives in the Rome of the past and the

future, the Rome that is eternal and un-
changing.

He lives in and for the Rome that during a century and a half of unrelenting
warfare subdued the hardy cohorts of the
ancestors of the present-day Italians, and
with them, after she had enrolled them
under her standards, took possession of the
entire world in less than a century. He lives
in and for the Rome that later, bearing the
Gospel of Christ, wandered anew through
the world on her mission of unification. He
lives in and for the Rome that again spread
her new-found culture over the world when
the glorious period of the Renaissance created civilization out of medieval barbarism
and unified the earth for the third time.

In Rome, he feels all of the terrific responsibility of his destiny, which is the destiny of a people oppressed by the burden of
its glory and longing to march forth once
more on its mission of wisdom and valor.

Under the vigilant gaze of this new

Leader, the ancient rebels bow their heads and in unremitting toil find again the Fatherland that they had lost in the fearful disorder of a day. The inflexible will of the man who emerged from the trenches where the Italian people left the flower of their youth has already given them, and the entire Italian people with them, the ancient Roman Fatherland.

In his hands are the destinies of Italy, perhaps of Europe.

No one, not even the most irreconcilable of his foes, can deny today the existence of a new, youthful Italian spirit, the work of Mussolini, who led a revolution that is without parallel in history because it was bloodless.

This man's name is on everyone's lips today. The world follows his doings with curiosity, with admiration, sometimes with fear.

They call him Caesar, Napoleon, Cromwell, Robespierre, but he cares little; the son

[ 221 ]

of a blacksmith, intent upon the work of re-
storing to Italy the form, substance and
spirit that will again make her great and
mighty among the nations, he is satisfied with
being, for the present, simply Benito
Mussolini.

N